# ACTIVATE YOUR HIGHEST POTENTIAL WITH SACRED GEOMETRY

## A Practical Guide to Freedom, Authenticity and Fulfilment

by
**Sabine Kruse**

**SPOTLIGHT**
PUBLISHING HOUSE

*Goodyear, AZ U.S.A.*

Published by Spotlight Publishing House™, United States of America
https://spotlightpublishinghouse.com

Editing: Janet Swift of Swiftly Sorted, Gloucestershire, UK – janetswiftauthor@gmail.com
Cover Design: Danijel Trstenjak, Gaialit, Slovenia, https://gaialit.com
Interior Design: Marigold2k

ACTIVATE YOUR HIGHEST POTENTIAL WITH SACRED GEOMETRY – A Practical Guide to Freedom, Authenticity and Fulfilment / Sabine Kruse

First Edition

Ebook ISBN: 978-1-958405-77-2
Paperback ISBN: 978-1-958405-78-9
IngramSpark Paperback ISBN: 978-1-958405-92-5
IngramSpark Hardcover ISBN: 978-1-958405-90-1

# Contents

## Part III

# Part IV

# Endorsements

If you've been wondering how to navigate a complicated and ever-changing world, this brilliant book, infused with ancient wisdom, is the key. Beginning with an extensive overview of geometric shapes and how to use them, the author then shares practices to activate your highest potential, increase energy and abundance, as a foundation for meditation and contemplation or even to raise the frequency in meetings. It's a game changer!

**Andrea Hylen**
Founder of Heal My Voice and The Incubator: An online co-working space for cultural creatives

The world has been waiting for this book for the longest time! The practical, interesting and informative exercises using sacred geometry will keep you returning to its pages time and time again. Sabine has given us a gift which not only takes you to your highest potential but will also have a knock-on effect on your loved ones, colleagues and people you come in contact with.

**Danielle M Helms**
Light Worker, Yoga Teacher and Sacred Earth Practitioner

This book is an excellent avenue for opening the portals to energetic majesty. After introducing the basic information around various sacred geometric shapes and colors, we are treated to hands-on methods to positively accentuate situations presenting in our lives, carrying us ever higher on our pathways to living more fulfilling, abundant and peace-filled lives. Sabine masterfully shows us we can easily utilize these gorgeous, code-carrying sacred geometry figures to uplift us and magnify our personal and collective magnificence throughout each day.

**LouAnne Ludwig**
Author & Master Intuitive
*www.LouAnneLudwig.com*

In this book, Sabine opens a valuable door on how the Universe communicates in shapes. With the suggested exercises, you can feel a difference in your state of being immediately and gain accelerated insights in a matter of minutes. Use these powerful tools for tapping into divine guidance so you can embrace the challenges and questions which present along life's path. I highly recommend it.

**Monisha Mittal**
Somatic Coach and Founder of Big Love Alchemy

Immediately hooked by the cogent information within sacred geometry, the real integration into cellular biology just blew me away. As a medical professional and seasoned traveller, I found the practical implications for healing easy to understand and used the geometric symbols to reinvigorate and heal my body in various settings. Providing a rich blend of ancient wisdom, the author explores how consciousness connects us with many mind-blowing interconnected layers of universal information, concluding with the understanding that we can transform our own lives and help co-create and inform the world around us. A truly illuminating and inspiring read that I recommend to anyone interested in sacred geometry.

**Lesley A Graham RN**
Author and Speaker

Empowering and magical! It's a wonderful gift to have a book so easy to read and comprehend while activating many soulful reconnections and remembrances in a playful way. Are you ready to awaken those divine codes and frequencies vibrating at the core of your soul and to expand your consciousness beyond your perceived limits? Working with sacred geometry, is it time to step into your own divinity? If yes, then go for it! Open your heart, mind, and soul and dive into the magical pages of this book. Your transformational journey awaits!

**Shuntena**
Cosmic Shaman

I have heard and read about sacred geometry for many years, but while going through Sabine's pioneering work, I was struck by how little I truly knew about the subject. As I turned the pages and studied the fascinating images, I was delighted to discover the practical application to everyday life. Sabine's wisdom and knowledge of the subject is quite impressive. I will reread this book and use it as a resource to implement what I have learned. What timely information for our out-of-balance world!

**Becky Norwood**
Author of The Woman I Love, CEO of Spotlight Publishing House

# Dedication

I dedicate this book to the True Self in each and every one of us.
May we shine brightly!

SABINE KRUSE

# Preface

Figure 1: 8-pointed star cupola in the Alhambra Palace in Granada/Spain

## How and why I came to write this book

Have you ever wondered how you can contribute to creating a peaceful, free, abundant and beautiful world? I know I have.

Growing up in Germany in the '70s and '80s, I felt an innate desire to explore and understand the world. Why is there so much poverty and inequality? How do we find peace amidst conflict and war? How can we thrive amid all the rules, limitations and expectations? What do I have to do to fit in? Have you ever asked yourself these or similar questions?

After studying economics in England to learn more about the concept of abundance, I worked for 20 years in development co-operation programmes aimed at improving socio-economic, political and environmental conditions in Africa and Latin America. Although I enjoyed working with people around the world while looking for solutions for a better life for everyone, satisfying answers eluded me. Instead, I came to realise that you cannot change the world from the outside. A deep inner knowing that life offered more than I was experiencing and witnessing in others led me to leave my corporate job in 2011.

Guided by my intuition and propelled forward by my curiosity about the purpose of life, I embarked upon a journey of self-awareness, exploring my soul and inner realms through meditations and spiritual programmes.

Towards the end of 2014 sacred geometry came into my life. I began regularly experimenting with well-known sacred geometry shapes and forms, exploring their energetic qualities and effects upon me. Around the same time, I started working with Jennifer Hough, founder of The Wide Awakening, in a programme to activate my innate abilities and multidimensional superpowers.[1]

Six months later, Thoth showed up as my guide. Thoth is a multi-faceted being: In Ancient Egypt, Thoth – often depicted with a human body and the head of an ibis – was revered as the god of writing, geometry, magic and wisdom. He is also known as the Greek Hermes Trismegistus who discovered alchemy and was a messenger of the gods and author of sacred texts. The essence of Hermes' teachings is laid out in the 7 Hermetic Principles, the laws governing our world and the universe. Thoth is also said to have lived as a wise priest king in Atlantis. At the end of Atlantis, he secured the ancient wisdom for a time when humanity was ready to receive it again.

In the summer of 2015, while participating in a seminar where a tetrahedron was used to bring about desirable shifts in our energy fields, I suddenly received a message from Thoth through a kind of telepathic communication. Thoth invited me to do a ceremony with

---

[1]  https://thewideawakening.com/innate-abilities-home-study/

a friend during which he would advise me how to reconnect 12 pieces of innate abilities and ancient knowledge that had been spread out among 12 people at the end of Atlantean times. At first, I wasn't sure whether I was imagining it or whether it was really happening. In the end, my curiosity won over my doubts and I decided to give it a go. Together with my friend – and in soul connection with the other ten people – I followed Thoth's instructions and felt his energetic presence throughout the process. At the end, I saw an image of the Great Pyramid of Giza in Egypt in my mind's eye. For quite some time, I didn't know what this was all about.

After Thoth's first contact, I continued receiving information during meditations on how to use certain geometric shapes and forms to shift the underlying energetics for everyday issues in order to create tangible results in daily life. I began writing down these insights and short practices, remembering how much I enjoyed doodling spheres and cubes in my notebooks at secondary school. Both forms are still very useful today: The sphere is a symbol of creation, and the cube supports manifesting your heart-based desires in the material world.

My engagement with sacred geometry gained momentum when I moved from Germany to Granada/Spain in early 2018. Sacred geometry in the designs of tiles and on pavements in the city of Granada, as well as in the famous Alhambra Palace, surrounded me from then on. On one of my first visits to the Alhambra Palace, I marvelled at the beauty and exquisite energy of the artfully carved and painted designs, basking in the beauty of the stars of various shapes and sizes on the walls, tiles and ceilings. A main element of the Islamic heritage in southern Spain is the 8-pointed star. You will also find other sacred geometric designs such as the 16-pointed star, the 10-pointed star and the Tree of Life. The Alhambra Palace's Hall of the Abencerrajes displays a beautiful three-dimensional cupola of 8-pointed stars (see Figure 1) that come down in layers from the ceiling and end in the cubical base of the hall. I felt the expansive energy of the stellar upper part of the hall ("connection to the heavens above") and the grounding energy of the cubical lower part of the hall ("connection to Earth"). Needless to say, I became a regular visitor to the Alhambra Palace.

While I was exploring sacred geometry in Granada, Thoth stepped forward again – this time as my overall mentor for this book. I connected with him and other guides on a regular basis to receive guidance and insights – wisdom from Ancient Egypt, the pyramids, sacred geometry as well as the Hermetic Principles and their applications in everyday life. Thoth offered to energetically infuse this book with the wisdom of the 7 Universal Laws, the so-called 7 Hermetic Principles, symbolised by the 7-pointed star on the book cover. The cover's spiralling white spheres against a cosmic background represent to me the journey of the soul from Source through the cosmos to Earth.

Step-by-step, this book took shape. I've played with the short practices in Chapter 7 many times, using them on myself and with friends, family and clients. During these years, I went through the process of freeing myself from my limitations and conditioning, returning to being natural and authentic. I shifted from living life from my mind to living life from my heart and soul – a much more fulfilling experience.

The famous words of Mahatma Gandhi "Be the change you wish to see in the world" catalysed my understanding that focusing on peace, gratitude and the beauty of life in our inner experience is the most effective way to experience peace, joy and beauty in the outer world. By becoming fully aware of ourselves, our human nature as well as our true nature, we can step beyond our limitations and conditioning and live the best possible life. Engaging with and experiencing sacred geometry assists us in doing exactly that!

## Scope of this book

According to my research, most publications on sacred geometry deal with the beauty of the shapes and forms, their occurrences in nature and the cosmos, architectural designs and/or the mathematical, numerological and scientific properties of sacred geometry. There is little published information on the energetic properties and everyday use of sacred geometry shapes and forms, other than some books focusing on one or a few main shapes and forms such as the Flower of Life, the Merkaba and the Platonic solids. In this sense, this book is unique and needs to be written.

Every sacred geometry shape or form has specific underlying energetic qualities. I use the word "shape" to refer to a two-dimensional representation of a sacred geometry image (a plane measured by length and width), such as a triangle or a square, instead using the word "form" to refer to a three-dimensional representation (a solid measured by length, width and height) such as a tetrahedron or a cube. Such energetic qualities can be used to address a topic you may be dealing with. Let me give you an example: If you're experiencing heightened emotions, I'm going to show you which shape or form could help you and how you can use it to return to (a higher degree of) emotional balance and stability.

**The structure of the book is as follows:**

Part I sets the context for this book and provides an overview of the nature of sacred geometry and its purpose. Part II presents the main sacred geometry shapes and forms and the stars with varying numbers of points, describing their geometries, energetic qualities and utilisations and facilitating your first energetic experience with each shape or form.

Part III is where the rubber meets the road: It inspires you to use sacred geometry in the ways that resonate most with you – and to start playing! Chapter 7 is the heart of this book, consisting of many practices for all kinds of topics and providing tools to create solutions and tangible results in your daily life.

Part IV contains a synopsis of my series on the 7 Hermetic Principles, final words, a bibliography and useful links as well as previews of my next two sacred geometry books. At the end, you'll find acknowledgments and further information. Just before finalising this book, Thoth stepped in with an afterword. Of course, it had to be Chapter 13! If you wonder why, check the significance of the number "13" outlined in Chapter 4.9 on Metatron's Cube.

## Reading tips

Please note that I use the terms "Source", "Creator", "Spirit", "ALL THAT IS" and "Divine" interchangeably throughout the book – depending on the focus I want to portray. What I refer to is the infinite, eternal, limitless, all-knowing One that cannot be explained in words and can only be experienced to a certain degree. Some of you might want to call it "God" – the God of your understanding – "the Universe", "Existence", "(Universal) Love" or "(Universal) Consciousness". Please feel free to replace my terms with the word(s) that feel(s) most comfortable to you.

I also use the terms "soul", "essence", "Higher Self", "I AM Presence" and "True Self" interchangeably, referring to the divine spark and eternal part within us, which is a part and unique expression of Source/Creator/Spirit/the Divine. Again, I invite you to use the term(s) that resonate(s) most with you.

When I use the expression "step into the sacred geometry by intention", I mean "say or think: I set the intention to step into the sacred geometry." Your focused intention then informs your energetic system about what you want to experience. Energy follows intention and attention.

Feel free to engage with this book in any order you like. You might want to read it all from beginning to end if you wish to become acquainted with the nature of sacred geometry and its potential utilisations. Or you might be interested in specific shapes and forms, in which case you could refer directly to the chapters providing you with the corresponding information and practices. If you are dealing with a specific concern or objective, you might wish to directly consult the topic-related practices in Chapter 7, offering tailor-made solutions.

Please know the information I present comes through me and has been confirmed by my experiences with myself, clients and others. This is MY truth, not THE truth. As the reader, I encourage you to feel into which parts of the information resonate with you and invite you to focus on those, discarding the ones which do not. Please make this choice from YOUR inner truth and not from the limited perspective of your brain. Connecting to your zero-point will assist you with this process (see Chapter 4.0).

I truly wish for you to enjoy this book! May the practices support you in activating your highest potential as they have supported me and many others, empowering you to experience more freedom, authenticity and a fulfilled life!

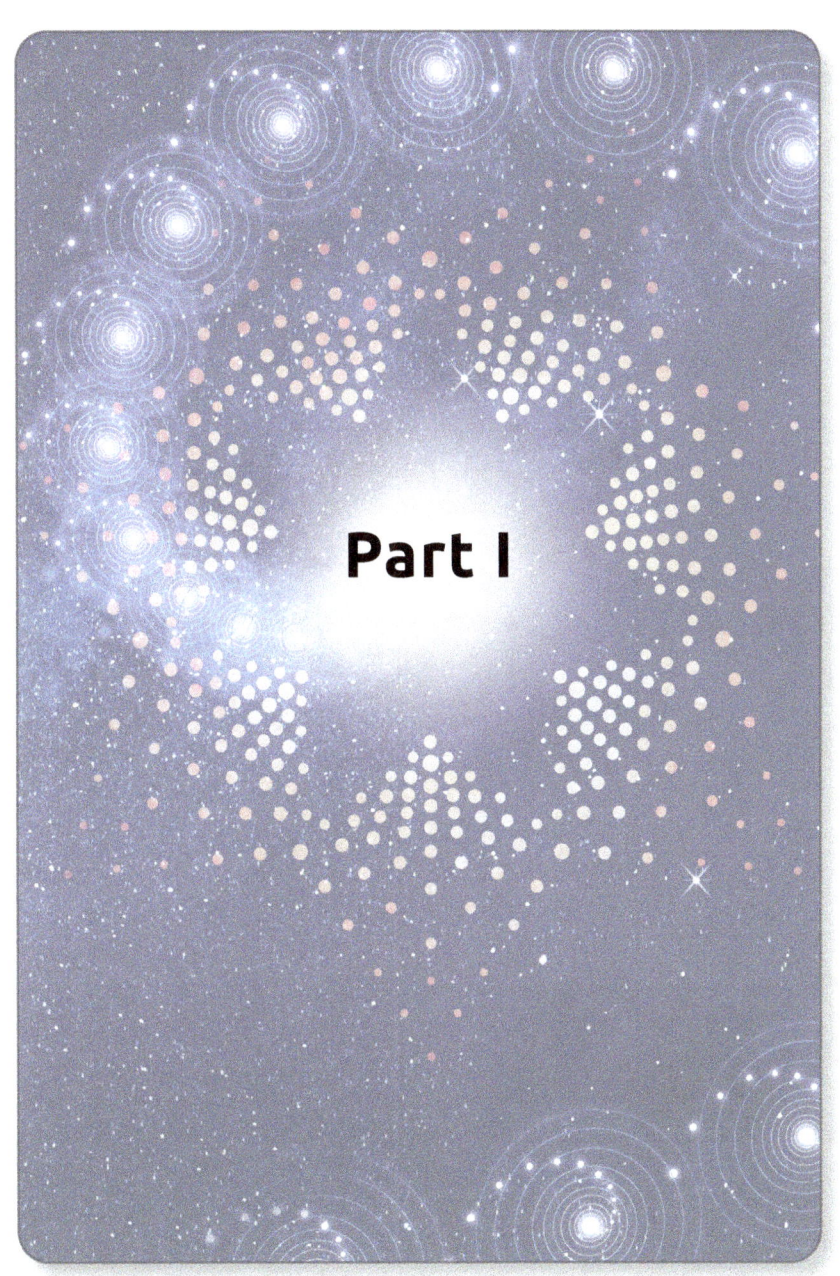

# Part I

# Chapter 1

# Introduction

Figure 2: Essence Flower

## 1.1
## Message from the Author

*"Geometry will draw the soul toward truth."*
Plato (Greek philosopher, 427-347 BC)

Are you living your highest potential?

Or do you know deep inside that there is more to life than your job, your daily routine and what you are experiencing in the world around you?

Our life situations happen thanks to 90-95% of our subconscious and unconscious programmes, beliefs, (suppressed) emotions and experiences. Our subconscious minds are much more powerful than our conscious minds and gear us towards surviving rather than thriving. Our parents' beliefs and experiences programmed our subconscious since conception, and later, other people and society influence us. These programmes trigger thoughts and emotions and activate biological and chemical processes in our bodies and energy systems with corresponding effects on our well-being and our lives in general. The subconscious also holds valuable information about our abilities and experiences, which we can unlock.

Our world is as we are. If we are riddled with doubt, fear or lack, we cannot live our highest potentials. Engaging with sacred geometry can change that, simply by looking at it, since its information is directly absorbed by our subconscious without being filtered by the left hemisphere of the brain, our rational minds. Through its inherent divine codes, sacred geometry supports us in freeing our subconscious of conditioning and programming – the emotions, limiting beliefs and patterns we are not (consciously) aware of – thereby facilitating the experience of our essence.

Activating your highest potential is about activating/remembering your essence, your True Self. Living your life from your True Self, which is deeply connected to your heart, rather than from your programmed mind and ego will lead you to freedom, authenticity and fulfilment.

Everything you need is within you. You are the master of your life; this book's information and tools are here to support you. The heart of this book contains many inspirational practices meant to empower you to raise your awareness and create tangible results in your daily life.

This could mean:

- Regaining emotional balance
- Restoring peace of mind

- Finding clarity
- Building up confidence to move ahead in life
- Increasing your energy and well-being

The variety and simplicity of practices for everyday topics pick you up where you are at every moment.

The unique frequencies embedded in each geometric shape and form bring about certain energetic changes. Take the example of the image called "Essence Flower" in Figure 2, which I also use as my logo together with my name: It contains the frequencies of freedom (infinity symbols in gold), authenticity (7-pointed star in green for being natural and in alignment with natural and cosmic laws) and fulfilment (golden sphere of wholeness encompassing all kinds of geometric shapes).

I have gone on this path, using these practices over and over again for myself as well as with family, friends and clients during my coaching sessions and webinars. I am very grateful for the favourable shifts and tangible results I witnessed in myself and others, freeing us of limitations, old patterns and emotions, (re-)connecting us to our True Selves and facilitating the lives we want to live.

If you feel or know it is time to step into a new life and you are looking for effective tools and compassionate guidance from someone who has gone on this path before, this book is for you. Sacred geometry takes you home to your soul, to your unique divine blueprint. I am delighted to support you in remembering your True Self, the love that you are. Are you ready?

# 1.2
# Message from Thoth
(as telepathically received by the author)

Figure 3: Image of Thoth on a wall at the temple of Ramses II in Abydos/Egypt

Dear Reader,
Are you ready to step into your highest potential?

Welcome to the world of sacred geometry and to its experiential realms! Welcome to the world of limitless possibilities and potentials. Welcome to YOU, to whom you really are.

Welcome to this book! I encourage you to play with the information in these pages. Let it play with you. See it as a dance. Some sacred geometry shapes and forms will appeal to you more than others and some tools you might want to incorporate as daily practices for some time. There will be other tools and pieces of information that do not resonate with you. All is well. Please know that sacred geometry is becoming more important in these times of rapid change. You will experience its power and possibilities more and more in the years to come.

As a mentor and friend of the author, I energetically infused this book with my wisdom, knowledge and teachings from the 7 Hermetic

Principles, universal laws that govern your Earth, the cosmos and the whole universe. These Hermetic Principles are embedded in the symbol of the 7-pointed star on the book cover to support you, the reader, in understanding and relating to the laws of the universe on conscious and subconscious levels. The author has published a series on the 7 Hermetic Principles on Instagram which forms part of this book.

My dearest wish is for you to utilise the material the author has presented in such a precise and loving way so that you can remember your True Self and activate your highest potential. The book is written in a very practical way to empower you to take from it what you need and what most serves you. It does not require any background knowledge in mathematics, sacred geometry or in any spiritual practices and teachings. The author has infused the corresponding sacred geometry shapes and forms with her knowledge, wisdom and frequencies, not only from her human self but also from her multidimensional self and from her essence as a soul.

By the word "multidimensional" I mean to say that you are so much more than just a three-dimensional human being. You are having a human experience right now, but you are so much more: You have lived in, and experienced, so many other realms and dimensions. I leave it to you to find out what your multidimensionality is and to experience it. Let me say that much at this point: You – as well as every other living being – is Source energy and has come from, and is an expression of, the Creator itself. This is embedded in the first Hermetic Principle: "THE ALL is mind." This principle also contains the truth: "While All is in THE ALL, it is equally true that THE ALL is in All."

You are told by many of your scientists that you only have a double-stranded DNA[2] and that only a small part of your DNA is functional with instructions and genetic information, while the remaining

---

[2]  Deoxyribonucleic Acid

75-98% of your DNA is "junk DNA". How could it be so? Let me ask you: If you were to create something, would you come up with a design where the vast majority of the blueprint had no function and was simply useless? How much of the design and operating system of your cars has no purpose at all? And do you believe that the Creator of human beings was so ignorant or so careless as to create a blueprint, which is largely deficient or useless? Remember, Human, remember! Your so-called "junk DNA" is not junk at all. It contains your multidimensional facets where your highest potential lies. Let us activate it now! It is time.

I am honoured to support you on your journey home to your divine origin and True Self. I am honoured to have co-created this book with the author, my dear friend, Sabine. May it serve you to activate your highest potential and lead you to freedom, authenticity and a fulfilled life!

With love and gratitude,

THOTH
alias HERMES TRISMEGISTUS

# Chapter 2

# What is Sacred Geometry?

Figure 4: Nautilus shell fossil

Did you know that the whole universe is built on sacred geometry – nature, the cosmos as well as the human body? You and I are based on sacred geometry. Everything is composed of geometry in varying forms, shapes, colours, sequences and directions.

**Golden ratio, Fibonacci sequence and zero-point**

"Geometry" comes from two Greek words meaning, "measuring Earth". The word "sacred" refers to the fact that this type of geometry is all-embracing and follows divine principles of proportion and direction. The so-called "golden ratio" (or "golden mean") reflects this sacredness. The golden ratio displays perfectly harmonic proportions found at the origin of all life which speak to the soul through their inherent beauty. In short, the golden ratio is a mathematical ratio defining true beauty and harmony. The proportions in a beautiful human face, a flower petal and an exquisite piece of art, music or architecture contain approximations of the golden ratio. Your soul is attracted to these expressions of true beauty and harmony, reminding you of your divine origin and uplifting your human experience.

Let's look at the mathematical ratio for true beauty: A ratio of a line divided into two unequal parts a and b is called the "golden ratio" φ (Greek letter "phi")[3] when the entire line (a+b) divided by the longer part (a) is equal to the longer part (a) divided by the shorter part (b), resulting in the infinite number of 1.61803…: φ = (a+b)/a = a/b = 1.61803…

The Fibonacci sequence is the underlying principle of the golden ratio. It was introduced to Europe by the Italian mathematician Leonardo Bonacci or Fibonacci who lived in the Republic of Pisa in the 12th/13th century.[4]

The Fibonacci sequence is made up of an infinite sequence of numbers where each number is formed by adding the previous two numbers: 0; 1; 1; 2; 3; 5; 8; 13; 21; 34; 55; 89; 144; …

In detail: 0+1=1; 1+1=2; 1+2=3; 2+3=5; 3+5=8; 5+8=13; 8+13=21; 13+21=34; 21+34=55; 34+55=89; 55+89=144; …

One could say that by adding the past (number) to the present (number), you get to the future (number) – a metaphor for evolution. The ratio of the higher and lower of any two adjacent numbers (starting with 5/3; then 8/5; 13/8…) is approximately the golden ratio φ (phi) = 1.61803398….

---

[3]  The capital letter Φ is sometimes used as a symbol for the golden ratio, too.
[4]  https://en.wikipedia.org/wiki/Fibonacci

Notice the approximations of a golden spiral in Figure 5 below. A (logarithmic) spiral is called a "golden spiral" if it gets wider by the golden ratio factor of φ = 1.618… for every quarter-circle turn it makes. The "Fibonacci spiral" approximates a golden spiral, created by drawing circular arcs that connect the opposite corners of squares in the Fibonacci tiling. The lengths of the sides of the squares follow the numbers in the Fibonacci sequence referred to above.[5]

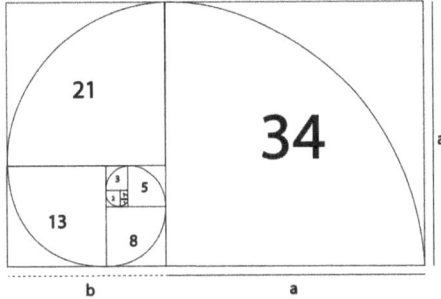

Figure 5: Fibonacci spiral

The Fibonacci sequence and spiral are ever expanding – just like the outward movement of the universe. This expansion occurs just like an explosion from the zero-point (0) of creation onwards.

Your zero-point can be viewed as the access point to your soul or essence. When I consciously breathe into the middle of my chest with the intention of going into my zero-point, I feel my essence and my connection to Source, to ALL THAT IS. I immediately become calm and centred. When I then set the intention of calling all my energies and aspects back home to my zero-point, I feel an incoming stream of energies and an expansion in my chest.

To get to the zero-point takes decision and focus: Decide to go to your zero-point and put your awareness and focus on the zero-point in the middle of your chest. Consciously breathing into this point

---

[5]   https://en.wikipedia.org/wiki/Golden_spiral

supports the experience. The zero-point reflects the number "0" of the Fibonacci sequence, the beginning of the golden spiral, the void of creation. In the infinity symbol, the zero-point can be seen as the point in the middle where the two loops cross.

**The number Pi (π)**

Another important number in sacred geometry is the number Pi (π). The underlying mathematics of circles and spheres (surface, area, volume, circumference) contain the infinite number π = 3.14... Circles and spheres represent creation and the nothingness at the origin of creation at the same time. The Greek mathematician and physicist Archimedes was the first to document Pi.[6]

**Sacred geometry in nature, the cosmos and the human body**

Figure 6: Pinecone

Let's return to the golden ratio and the Fibonacci spiral. The golden ratio is, for example, apparent in snowflakes, flower petals and water crystals. Its frequencies can also be experienced in certain works of art, architecture and music compositions. The Fibonacci spiral is visible in all forms of nature – from the nautilus shell, snails, pinecones, sunflowers and a Romanesco broccoli to the tail of a sea horse and the molecules of your DNA.

---

[6] In my next book on sacred geometry, Pi will be explored in more detail (see preview in Chapter 11).

The golden ratio is equally present in the cosmos, reflected within the constellations of stars, in the form of galaxies, the molecular structure of planets, the orbits of the planets in our solar system, the spiralling winds of a hurricane right down to the depths of Earth's oceans – and in everything in between.

Figure 7: Hurricane

I invite you to look out for patterns of sacred geometry in all forms of nature around you. For inspiration, please go to my Instagram page[7] where I posted a series with photos about sacred geometry in nature (photos from 16.07.2019 to 30.09.2019).

Our body is inherently symmetrical, too. The distance between your middle fingers of both hands at outstretched arms is approximately the same as the height of your body from head to foot. The golden ratio is present all over the human body. Let's look at some examples:

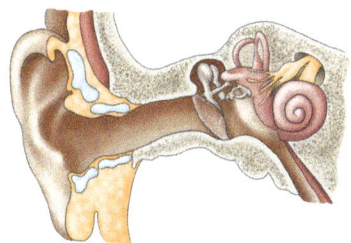

Figure 8: Human ear with inner spiral

---

[7]   https://www.instagram.com/sacredgeometryexperience/

- The human inner ear spiral reflects the Fibonacci spiral.
- The DNA molecule measures 34 angstroms[8] long by 21 angstroms wide for each full cycle of the double helix spiral (34/21 is approximately equal to φ = 1.618…).
- The ratio of the length of your forearm (a) to the length of your hand (b) approximates φ. The same is true for the proportion of the length of your forearm plus the length of your hand (a+b) to the length of your forearm (a): φ = a/b = (a+b)/a = 1.61803….
- The ratio of the length of your shin (a) to the length of your foot (b) approximates φ. You get the same result when you divide the sum of the length of your shin and the length of your foot (a+b) by the length of your shin (a): φ = a/b = (a+b)/a = 1.61803….

I invite you to try it out for yourself by measuring your own body proportions. If you're interested in finding out more, you'll find corresponding images and further evidence available online.

Sacred geometry is a foundational structural element in a universe, which is fractal. The term "fractal" was coined by the mathematician Benoît Mandelbrot and describes "…an object or quantity that displays self-similarity, in a somewhat technical sense, on all scales. The object need not exhibit exactly the same structure at all scales, but the same "type" of structures must appear on all scales…".[9] You can see fractal patterns following the rules of repetition and self-similarity in the cosmos and in nature such as in an uncurling fern leaf or the branching system of a tree or cloud. Perhaps you remember the Russian dolls – where several wooden dolls with the same characteristics and different sizes are stacked inside each other? Unified Physics studies the phenomenon of a fractal universe, showing us that "…the scale gradient from the tiniest to the largest dimensions in the universe is inherently fractal throughout…. Since we see similar geometries and patterns at vastly different scales in the

---

[8] An "angstrom" is a unit of length equal to one hundred-millionth of a centimetre.
[9] https://mathworld.wolfram.com/Fractal.html

universe, fractals can teach us how these scale layers interconnect".[10] This coincides with the Hermetic Principle of Correspondence: "As above, so below; as below, so above."

## Sacred geometry: the key to creation

In conclusion: Sacred geometry is the blueprint at the origin of our universe, nature and our bodies and is in everything in between. Sacred geometry is the universal language of the soul understood by all life which communicates on subconscious, cellular and atomic levels. By surpassing the filters of the programmed mind, sacred geometry powerfully and uninhibitedly delivers its divine codes to humans and any sentient being, reminding us of our common divine origin and our interconnectedness with all life. It helps our minds to perceive Spirit in action. This sacred geometry blueprint operates like a sun radiating out its light, its essence, through each and every one of its rays.

In other words, sacred geometry holds a certain frequency you pick up and resonate with like an antenna that catches a specific signal. Your body contains that frequency, and your soul resonates with it.

The ancient cultures knew about this. The Egyptians, Mayans and Celts built their monuments according to sacred geometry and taught its secrets in mystery schools dedicated to the learning of universal laws, mastery, magic, alchemy and all subjects which furthered the advancement of the soul, rather like "Hogwarts" in Harry Potter! Crop circles – large geometric patterns of flattened crops mostly found in fields in southern England – often also display sacred geometry patterns and frequencies.

In an interconnected and fractal universe where everything around us is energy brought into form (in-form-ation), sacred geometry expresses

---

[10] Resonance Science Foundation, Unified Science Course, Chapter 4.1.4 Fractal Universe at https://www.resonancescience.org/academy

divine codes and frequencies in geometric shapes and forms. Certain sacred geometry shapes and forms carry certain frequencies and types of consciousness that facilitate specific energetic and vibratory changes when you connect and engage with them. This book will show you the underlying energetic qualities of different shapes and forms. Sacred geometry is the key to creation. The golden ratio φ is the key to your multidimensionality where all realities co-exist.

**Different expressions of sacred frequencies and codes**

This book focuses on sacred geometric shapes and forms as well as related resources, tools and practical applications. To set the context, let me briefly talk about other expressions of sacred frequencies and codes.

Sacred frequencies and codes can be expressed in:

- Geometric shapes & forms
- Colours and combinations of colours (light codes)
- Sound & language (acoustic codes)
- Numbers & numeric codes
- Movements & rotations, particularly in combination with geometric shapes and forms
- Body movements and hand gestures (mudras)
- A combination of the above-mentioned elements

Colours influence your conscious and subconscious mind. When playing with the sacred geometry shapes and forms as shown in the following chapters, you might want to choose specific colours or observe which colours present themselves during the process. For practical purposes and to allow for neutrality, the images of sacred geometry shapes and forms in this book in general contain a black and white colouring. In some cases, I have added a coloured photo or image for a particular shape or form.

When using sacred geometry shapes and forms, you might also want to add or connect with any of the other expressions of sacred frequencies and codes mentioned above.

Apart from colours, I find movements particularly powerful. Sacred geometry shapes and forms do not tend to be static. Let them move, shift and rotate and see what changes. The rotation of a sacred geometry shape or form sets energetic shifts in motion. There are various types of rotations such as clockwise, anti-clockwise, backwards, forwards, tilted over a certain corner of the shape or form and spinning. Observe which rotation presents itself during your process. In my experience, anti-clockwise rotations tend to stir things up, bring them to the surface, clear and transmute them whereas clockwise rotations tend to bring in the new codes and restore the experience of divine order. However, there is some evidence that the direction of the rotation might differ for women and men – or for people with more feminine and more masculine energies. In other words, men – or people with more masculine energies – might experience clockwise rotations for clearing and transformation and anti-clockwise rotations for bringing in new codes. I invite you to experiment with it, following your intuition.

Certain sounds (such as gong, drumming and toning), light language, mudras, intuitive body movements and/or numeric codes might intensify the experiences with sacred geometry shapes and forms. I invite you to try it out as guided.

# Chapter 3

# What Purpose Does Sacred Geometry Serve?

Figure 9: Mosaic with 12-pointed star in Cyprus

*"If you want to find the secrets of the universe, think in terms of energy, frequency and vibration."*[11]
Nikola Tesla (inventor and engineer, 1856-1943)

Have you ever wondered why you have felt uplifted during a walk in a beautiful forest during springtime or while contemplating an exquisite piece of art, architecture or when listening to classical

---

[11] Energy is the inner flow of life force, enabling motion and activity. Vibration is the periodic back-and-forth movement around a point of equilibrium. Frequency is the rate at which energy vibrates. The higher the frequency, the more energy is brought through.

music? You have been touched by sacred geometry, the universal language of the soul.

Sacred geometry puts you into contact with your origin, your soul plan and the highest levels of creation. It supports you in accessing higher wisdom and potential, clearing blockages on all levels as well as restoring harmony in your physical body and energy system. It can be used as a tool to raise your awareness to know and embody the truth of who you are – on individual and collective levels. This is particularly important in the context of the parental, societal and religious conditioning we have received.

There is new scientific evidence and several recent scientific studies showing the impact of our thoughts and emotions as well as of frequencies we are exposed to in our personal lives and realities. For instance, Bruce Lipton demonstrates the impact of the mind on matter through the effects of our thoughts on our cells as well as the importance of the subconscious mind in creating our realities.[12] The noticeable impact of frequencies on the molecular structure of water has been demonstrated in Dr. Masaru Emoto's experiments on the messages from water.[13] Since on average more than 60% of our body is made up of water, any frequencies and codes we come into contact with influence our bodies and our lives.

That is why sacred geometry can assist you in freeing yourself from conditioning and limitations, in being authentic and in making your heart's dreams come true.

---

[12] Lipton, Bruce H.: The Biology of Belief, 2015. This book also contains references to several scientific studies to take you further on the subject of the (unconscious) mind and on DNA-related topics.

[13] The Japanese researcher, Dr. Masaru Emoto, exposed water in glasses to different types of music, thoughts and words, then froze the water and photographed the resulting ice crystals. The crystal patterns changed accordingly. For example, harmony and beauty were more evident in the crystal patterns if the water had been exposed to high vibrational (classical) music and "positive" uplifting words and thoughts.

**Use sacred geometry in your daily life to:**

- Activate your creative abilities and talents
- Unravel stuck energies and clear limiting patterns and beliefs
- Restore and increase vitality and well-being in your body and energetic system
- Sharpen your intuition and gain clarity, focus and new insights
- Restore emotional balance and develop amazing relationships with yourself and others
- Bring into your life what you truly desire from your heart
- Communicate with beings from higher dimensions
- Expand your consciousness allowing your True Self to emerge

**Two recommendations:**

1. This book is addressed to your soul – not to your rational mind. The limited perspective of the rational mind cannot grasp the full potential inherent in sacred geometry. I strongly encourage you to create an intuitive and visceral access to sacred geometry in order to experience its full benefits; feel and experience it, don't just "think" it! Visualise the sacred geometry (in action), feel or sense the sacred geometry in your body and energy system and watch or sense what opens up for you. As physicist Nassim Haramein states: "The atoms you are made of are 99.99999…% space, so the structure of space within your being is the structure of the unified field – and you are actually a manifestation of it."[14] If you have difficulties visualising, feeling or sensing the sacred geometry shapes and forms and their codes, just imagine you could see, feel or sense them. Experiencing sacred geometry will lead you to deep realisations of the interconnectedness of everything that will further your evolution. It's through becoming aware of all of you and by experiencing your emotions, feelings

---

[14] Resonance Science Foundation, Unified Science Course Virtual Series, Session 5: Module 5 – Ancient origins, minute 34:50 at https://www.resonancescience.org/academy

and bodily sensations that internal energetic shifts are made possible, not through your thoughts (alone). This is why this book focuses on the energetic qualities of sacred geometry as well as practical tools and experiences, rather than on the underlying mathematics and theoretical concepts.

2.  When you do the practices, be aware they might bring up old emotions, thoughts and beliefs stored in your body and mind as they are being released. You might also experience physical discomfort as your body sheds the old information. These practice-related effects usually last no longer than 24-48 hours. If they persist or if in doubt about their cause, always seek the advice of a physician or qualified health care professional regarding any mental, physical or emotional conditions you might encounter. Please be gentle with yourself; rest, relax and breathe, taking your time going through those processes. Stay hydrated and practice self-care perhaps by spending time in nature, taking a hot bath with Epsom salts, reading an uplifting book, getting enough rest and sleep and/or by doing something you enjoy and find helpful.

**A word of caution:**

Some people have manipulated some of the sacred geometry images used in the world for their own egoic purposes (such as power, greed and control). Tampering with sacred geometry is possible and has been done throughout the ages, just like you may have been influenced by programmes or parental conditioning, society and religious institutions, and language similarly has been misused for curses and verbal abuse. In other words, in a world of duality there are currently still forces at play, using "contaminated" sacred geometry shapes and forms for manipulation and control, but their reign of influence and impact is quickly vanishing. This does NOT mean that certain sacred geometry shapes and forms are inherently "negative" or "harmful". A manipulated sacred geometry shape or form can be restored to its original energy codes just by clear intention. If and when we use sacred geometry from the heart with pure intention and meaning for the highest and best good of all concerned, it remains pure. To support this purity, I recommend going into your zero-point at the beginning of each practice, which I explain in more detail in Chapter 4.0.

**A reminder:**

Sacred geometry is a powerful and easy-to-use tool. It can serve you very well when used from the intelligence of your heart and soul, rather than with your rational mind. When you use sacred geometry with love, the highest integrity and the purest intent, you can access its powerful codes and frequencies and your true potential and authentic power will continue to grow. This book has been written with pure intent from my soul for the highest and best good of all concerned.

May this book serve each and every one of you in remembering your True Self and activating your highest potential!

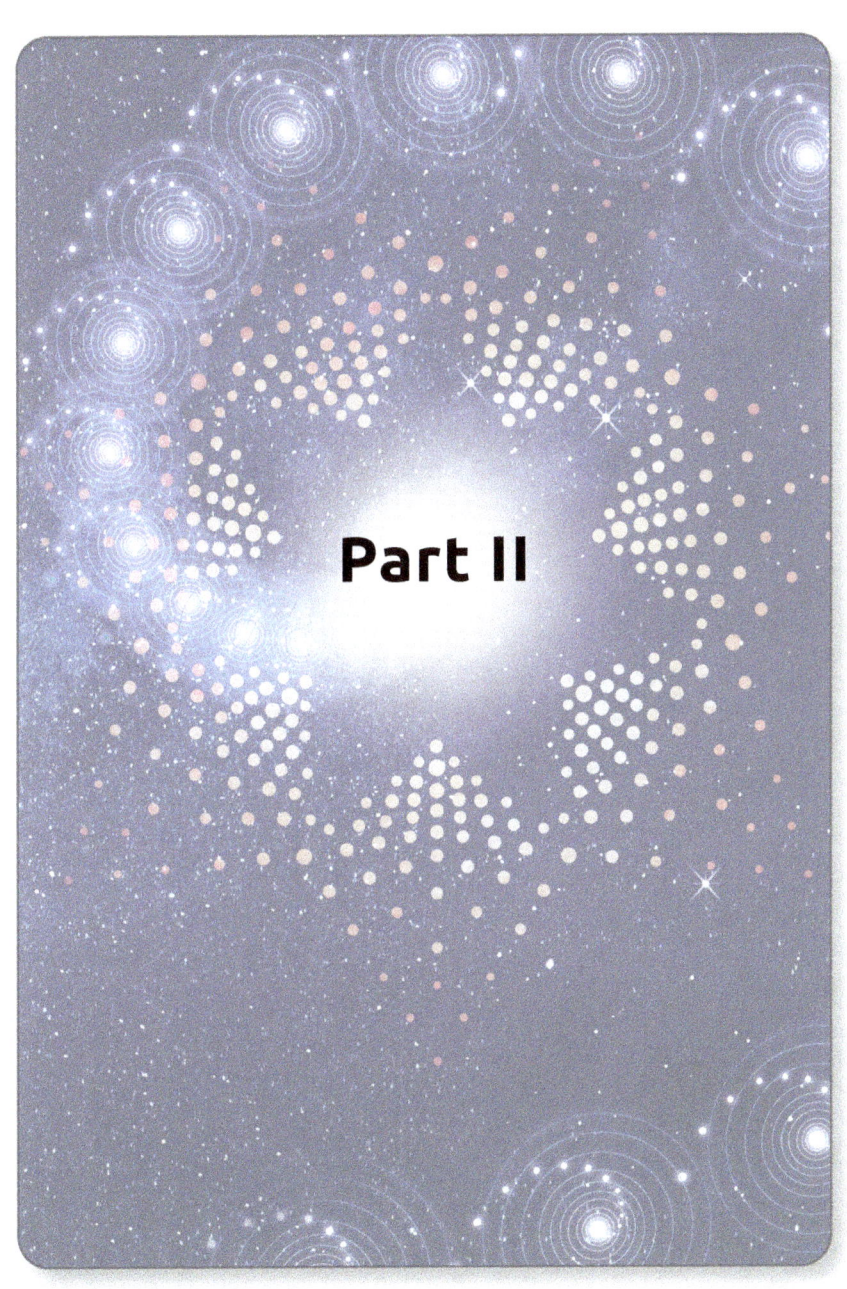

# Part II

# Chapter 4

# Overview of Foundational Sacred Geometry Shapes and Forms

Figure 10: Golden azeztulite sphere

In this chapter, you will get to know important and well-known sacred geometry shapes and forms, which I consider foundational for any sacred geometry engagement. I am going to present them with their energetic qualities and utilisations and invite you to explore their gifts through a first energetic experience. You may be familiar with some of the shapes and forms from noticing them in your surroundings or reading about them.

## Overview of foundational sacred geometry shapes and forms

The table below (see Figure 12) gives an overview of twelve foundational sacred geometry shapes and forms that can be related to the twelve chakras inside and outside the human body (see Figure 11).

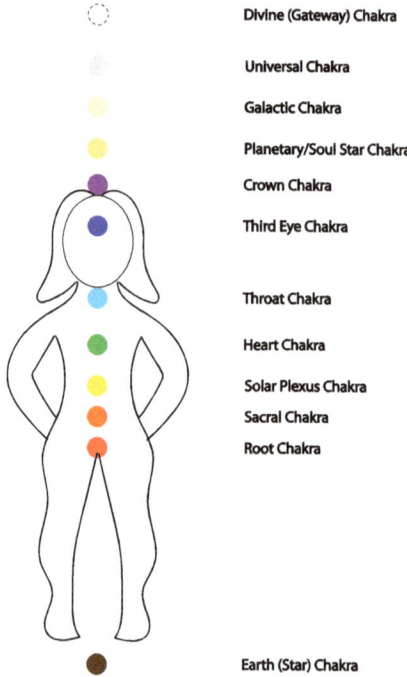

Figure 11: Twelve main chakras related to the human body

Chakras (Sanskrit for "wheel") are spinning energy centres in a human being that distribute the life force energy. The seven main chakras in a human body are located along the spinal column from the base of the spine to the crown of the head. There is also one main chakra about 45 cm or 18 inches below your feet – the Earth (star) chakra – as well as about four main chakras above the crown of your head.

The overview table (Figure 12) displays the sacred geometry shapes and forms, their names, focus and possible utilisations as well as their relationships to the twelve main chakras and where to find references to them. Where appropriate, their connections to the elements are also listed. The shapes and forms are presented in the order of the chakras from below to above the human body.

Beyond the physicality of the human body, there are various other layers – such as emotional, mental, etheric, astral, causal and auric – that form part of our wider energetic system. In this book, I will not go into detail about the different layers or bodies of the human energetic system, instead focusing on the physical body as well as the energetic body or energetic system of a human being. I use the terms "energetic body" and "energetic system" interchangeably in a comprehensive way, referring to all the different energetic layers in and around the human body that can be connected to an individual human being.

The information in the table is meant to serve as a reference and is based on my experiences when working with the twelve chakras.[15] It reflects what is congruent to me. This table is not meant to be comprehensive, nor to present THE truth. Again, I invite you to tune into what resonates with you.

---

[15] You can find additional information related to the five Platonic solids in German in the book "Die Heilige Geometrie der platonischen Körper" by Jeanne Ruland and Gudrun Ferenz (Schirner Verlag, 2014).

| Shape/ Form | Name | Chakra | Focus | Utilisations | Element | Main references in Chapters |
|---|---|---|---|---|---|---|
| Sphere | Sphere | Earth (Star) Chakra | Connection to Earth's life force | Zero-point connection; creation; insights | Crystal Kingdom | 4.1; 7.10; 11 |
| Hexa-hedron | Hexa-hedron | Root Chakra | Physical body | Grounding; bringing light into form; energy storage/ concentration | Earth | 4.6; 4.6.1; 7.1; 7.3; 7.10 |
| Icosa-hedron | Icosa-hedron | Sacral Chakra | Emotions | Emotional balance; release/ flow/renewal | Water | 4.6; 4.6.2; 7.2; 7.3; 7.10 |
| Tetra-hedron | Tetra-hedron | Solar Plexus Chakra | Energy levels | Raising energy and activity levels | Fire | 4.6; 4.6.3; 4.7; 7.3; 7.4; 7.10 |
| Octa-hedron | Octa-hedron | Heart Chakra | Mind | Clearing the old; making space for the new; clarity | Air | 4.5; 4.6; 4.6.4; 4.10; 7.5; 7.7; 7.10 |
| Dodeca-hedron | Dodeca-hedron | Throat Chakra | Conscious-ness | Opening up to higher guidance, universal love and grace | Ether | 4.6; 4.6.5; 5.1; 7.6; 7.10; 7.18 |
| Merkaba/ Star Tetra-hedron | Merkaba/ Star Tetra-hedron | Third Eye Chakra | Light body | Activating and expanding light body; harmonising polarities | Light | 4.7; 5.2; 7.7; 7.9; 7.14; 7.20 |

| | | | | | | |
|---|---|---|---|---|---|---|
| | Cosmic Egg | Crown Chakra | Revelation of Essence | Transformation; incubating and hatching the new | Essence | 4.8; 7.3; 7.7; 7.9; 7.13; 7.18 |
| | Metatron's Cube | Planetary/ Soul Star Chakra | Soul | Reinforcing soul plan on Earth; living your calling; focus; clarity | | 4.9; 7.8; 7.18 |
| | Diamond | Galactic Chakra | Multi-dimen-sional nature | Reflection of yourself in others; activation of multi-dimensional facets | | 4.10; 7.13; 7.14; 7.17; 9 |
| | Infinity Symbol | Universal Chakra | Infinite nature | Balancing opposites; full-circling experiences; relaxing into oneness | | 4.11; 7.16 |
| | Unbounded Flower of Life | Divine (Gateway) Chakra | Ever-expanding consciousness | Creating upon creation in divine order and harmony | | 4.12; 7.9; 7.12; 7.18 |

Figure 12: Overview of twelve foundational sacred geometry shapes and forms, their focus and utilisations as well as their relationships to the chakras

I invite you to check out my Instagram series on sacred geometries in relation to these twelve chakras with photos from 28.04.2019 to 07.07.2019.[16]

---

[16]  https://www.instagram.com/sacredgeometryexperience/

In Chapters 4.1 to 4.12 you will also find information on the following additional foundational sacred geometry shapes and forms (see Figure 13).

| Shape/ Form | Name | Focus | Utilisations | Comments | Main references in Chapters |
|---|---|---|---|---|---|
| | Vesica Piscis | Symbol of duality as well as balance of polar forces | Reflection on, and shift in, experience of opposites | Beginning of creation process: A single circle is divided into two circles | 4.2; 7.13 |
| | Trinity | Inter-connected-ness; eternal flow of life | Exploring the relationship dynamics among three people/ energies | Allows for third entity to emerge such as neutral observer of two opposites | 4.3; 7.13 |
| | Seed of Life | Seed of consciousness | Planting new seeds of creation | First flower element of the Flower of Life | 4.4 |
| | (Bounded) Flower of Life | Expanding consciousness (within certain boundaries) | Creating upon creation in divine order and harmony within a certain structure or form | Underlying pattern of creation of all physical forms | 4.4; 7.9; 7.12; 7.18 |
| | Pyramid | Energy storage, generation, amplification and transformation | Storing, gene-rating and amplifying energy; raising energy levels and vibrations | Similar to a tetrahedron but with a squared base | 4.5; 7.4; 7.11; 12 |
| | Fruit of Life | Fruit of Consciousness | Underlying structure for bearing the fruits of creation | Basis for Metatron's Cube | 4.9; 7.8; 7.18 |

Figure 13: Additional foundational sacred geometry shapes and forms

# 4.0
# Zero-Point Connection Tool

**Did you know that you have access to it all – from any place and at any time?**

Before diving into the details of sacred geometry, it's important to mention a powerful tool: the zero-point connection. I invite you to begin each of the practices by first connecting to your zero-point.

The zero-point is located in the centre of the heart chakra (see Figure 11) and is seen as the access point to the soul, to the quantum (unified) field – your connection to Source. It facilitates intuition and communication with realms beyond the three-dimensional experience in a body on planet Earth.

Please join me in a practice introducing you to ways of connecting to your zero-point: Take a few deep breaths. You might want to close your eyes. Imagine going down a golden spiral staircase all the way from your rational mind into the centre of your heart chakra. Focus on the location of your zero-point. Say or think: "I set the intention to connect to my zero-point" and breathe into it. Can you feel the connection to your soul, the universe and ALL THAT IS?[17]

Let me emphasise that you can connect to your soul and the quantum field in an instant, at any time you choose, wherever you are: Just intend to connect to your zero-point in the middle of your heart chakra, focus on it and breathe into it. Where attention goes, energy follows.

I invite you to do this practice at any time you feel imbalanced, worried, stressed, confused and/or overwhelmed. In my own experience, connecting to the zero-point immediately brings me back to my centre,

---

[17] Please refer to the video tutorials on my website for a guided experience into your zero-point connection.

to balance and presence. I also go into my zero-point before making a major decision. It is a reference point for neutrality and peace.

If you wish to remain present and connected to your soul and ALL THAT IS for longer periods of time, you might want to deal with the emotions, beliefs, thoughts and behavioural patterns that take you out of your zero-point and out of your peace and neutrality. The practices in this book will support you with this.

# 4.1
# Sphere

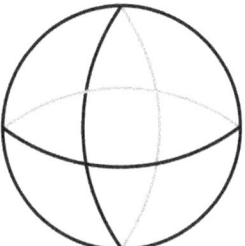

Figure 14: Sphere

## Description

When the (zero-) point expands in all directions, a circle emerges. It becomes a sphere in its three-dimensional representation (see Figure 14). The sphere is round without any edges or corners. It is the most efficient form in the sense that it has the least surface.

The sphere is the symbol of creation and, at the same time, the symbol of nothingness. It contains everything and nothing simultaneously. In other words, the sphere is the mother of all matter from which creation emerges – as well as the creation itself. In our earthly plane of existence, the sphere is connected to the Earth's life force and the Earth (star) chakra as well as the crystal kingdom. The sphere is also related to stillness, the zero-point and the number 0 as well as to the sound of creation "OM" and the "I AM Presence".

### Energetic qualities

Its energetic qualities can be defined as follows:

- Round, symmetrical
- Self-contained, complete
- Flexible, versatile
- Playful, inspiring you to play and explore

- Creative, fertile, birthing something new
- Still, peaceful
- Unifying, unity
- Representing fullness and nothingness at the same time

## Utilisations

The sphere offers energies of stillness and creativity and is particularly suitable for the following utilisations:

- Creation, creativity, birthing something new
- Fertility, abundance, vibrancy
- (Inner) Visions, insights, seeing the whole picture
- Supporting the inner child
- Harmonising topics related to "mother" such as the biological mother and Mother Earth

## Types of spheres for different perspectives and objectives

Different colours and degrees of density of the sphere offer different perspectives and objectives:

- A crystalline sphere supports you with insights and visions.
- A light-filled yellow or golden sphere reflects the Sun or the Creator itself. Use this type of sphere to initiate a creative endeavour.
- A lunar-white sphere representing the full moon can inspire your creation process from the planting of the seeds (new moon) to the opening of their blossoms (full moon).
- A sphere resembling planet Earth reflects fertility, abundance and vibrancy and can be used for topics related to your inner child and your mother/Mother Earth.

## Experience the sphere

Find a suitable sphere, hold it in your hands, perhaps rolling it around from time to time, and connect with it energetically. Go into your zero-point. Choose something you want to create or a topic you would like to be supported with. State your intention, for example: "I ask the sphere to support me in creating a new project xyz." Ask the sphere to show you insights and visions with respect to that topic. Close your eyes, feel the energy of the sphere, and be open to what shows itself in the form of an image, words or a feeling.

# 4.2
# Vesica Piscis

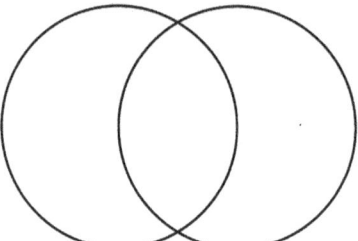

Figure 15: Vesica Piscis

## Description

The Vesica Piscis reflects the beginning of the process of creation, such as the cellular replication process for a human being: The single sphere (or circle) is divided into two spheres (or circles) to form a Vesica Piscis (see Figure 15). In its three-dimensional representation, the Vesica Piscis consists of two equal (in size and form) and independent spheres, which share an area of intersection in the middle. In its two-dimensional representation, you see two circles intersecting with each other in an eye-shaped or almond-shaped area.

The Vesica Piscis marks the beginning of separation from Source and reflects duality and polarity, in other words: I AM and YOU ARE. The Vesica Piscis is also a symbol of balance, balancing out the polar forces of its two equal sides. Seen as a mirror, the Vesica Piscis symbolises the reflection of yourself in somebody else or the reflection of the Creator in you. The intersection is the common area, which you can develop together and either choose to nurture or not.

Duality plays a necessary part in the evolution of consciousness. You come from oneness into duality to experience yourself through the other(s) before you return to unity and oneness by remembering your true nature and ending the projections onto others. I am going to share more about my view on the evolution of consciousness in Chapter 4.11 on the infinity symbol.

## Energetic qualities

The energetic qualities of the Vesica Piscis depend on which part of the geometry you focus on. If your focus is on the outer area of one circle (or sphere), you tend to feel the separation from the other circle (or sphere). By stepping into the intersection of the two circles (or spheres), you're likely to feel their balance and union – unity through diversity.

## Utilisations

Decide which perspective you want to take (outer circle/sphere or intersection) and which part of the process and momentum you wish to explore.

You can use the Vesica Piscis to reflect on your current experience of certain opposites in your life, for instance the relationships between you and your romantic partner, your True Self and your personality, your masculine and feminine sides or your inner and outer worlds. The Vesica Piscis also supports the shifting of perspectives on, and the underlying energetics of, these relationships.

## Experience the Vesica Piscis

Go into your zero-point. Choose the opposites you want to explore. Assign one circle of the Vesica Piscis to one of the opposites and the other circle to the other one. Imagine, sense or feel a Vesica Piscis in front of you. Ask it to show you through the sizes and forms of its two circles and their intersection how you are currently experiencing those polarities. Perceive the changes in the Vesica Piscis in front of you. Tune in: What kinds of sensations, thoughts, emotions or insights come up in your awareness? Step into the intersection of the circles by intention and experience your chosen opposites from that unifying perspective. In the experience of duality, can you find your way back to unity in the intersection area?

## 4.3
## Trinity and (Celtic) Triad

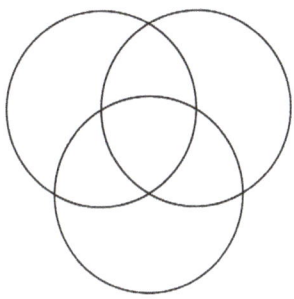

Figure 16: Trinity

Figure 17: Celtic
Triad/Triqueta

**Description**

The creation process continues with the introduction of a third sphere (or circle). Out of duality something new is born, which goes out into the world: The third entity.

The concept of trinity can be applied to various contexts, for instance:

- Mother, Father, Child
- I, the other (person), the Divine
- Trinity within us: Higher Self, Conscious Human Self and Sub-/ Unconscious Human Self
- Trinity within and around us: Universal Light/Source, (Etheric) Body, Soul (see Chapters 4.7 and 7.20 on the Merkaba)
- Two opposites and one neutral observer
- Trinity at the stage of oneness: Love, Lover and Beloved

The trinity is an important concept in many cultures. One familiar trinity symbol is the Celtic triad or triqueta (see Figure 17). It is based on the intersections of the three circles of the trinity symbol (see Figure 16) and consists of three half circles connected in an infinite loop with a circle going through them.

## Energetic qualities and utilisations

The trinity and (Celtic) triad symbols show the interconnectedness and the eternal flow of life and may be used to explore the following relationship dynamics:

- Union of two people or energies creating a third entity, which could be a relationship, a child or a project
- Universal light/Source, soul and body for a person
- Interconnectedness of all life
- Infinite loop of creation, eternal flow of life

## Experience the trinity

Again, go into your zero-point. Choose the polarities you want to explore as well as a potential third entity. You might first want to experience the Vesica Piscis as described in Chapter 4.2. Once you have (energetically) stepped into the intersection area of the Vesica Piscis, invite the third entity to join you. Explore the form, size and location of the third entity represented by the third circle. Step into the intersection of all three circles and experience the common area of your co-creation. What does it look like and how does it feel?

## 4.4
## Flower of Life

Figure 18: Seed of Life

Figure 19: (Bounded)
Flower of Life

**Creating the Flower of Life**

The creation process continues: If you keep adding partly overlapping circles of equal size around the central circle's intersection points with the other circles in a symmetrical fashion, you reach the first flower, which contains six circles around a central circle. This symbol is called the Seed of Life (see Figure 18).

By continuing to draw circles of equal size around the outer intersection points of any two circles, the Flower of Life is created (see Figure 19).

The Seed of Life and the Flower of Life can also be drawn with spheres instead of circles in their three-dimensional representations.

**Description**

The Flower of Life constitutes the underlying pattern of creation of all physical forms ("blueprint of creation") and the foundation of all existence. It reflects divine order and the interconnectedness of all life. Everything comes from it, and everything can be returned to it. Other sacred geometry shapes and forms, such as the five

Platonic solids, the Merkaba and Metatron's Cube, all derive from the Flower of Life. The Seed of Life is at the centre of this expansive consciousness.

The Flower of Life stores every experience, thought and feeling of every being and planet in the universe. Wisdom and insights are encoded in it. Every living being holds the crystalline structure of a Flower of Life within itself, connecting it to Source. Every Flower of Life in a living being (e.g. a human being) is connected to the Flower of Life in the centre of its home planet (e.g. Earth), which is connected to the Flower of Life in the centre of its Sun (e.g. Sun of our solar system), which in turn connects to the centre of the Central Sun of the universe.

The Flower of Life is normally displayed with two or three rings around the floral pattern (see Figure 19). In meditations I received insights about the unbounded Flower of Life and its importance in these times of expanding consciousness. This chapter focuses on the bounded Flower of Life whereas Chapter 4.12 deals with the unbounded Flower of Life.

**Energetic qualities**

The energetic qualities of the (bounded) Flower of Life can be defined as follows:

- Creative
- Symmetrical
- Harmonious
- Containing and spreading life force energy
- Expansive (within its boundaries)

## Utilisations

The Seed of Life assists in planting new seeds of creation. The Flower of Life supports creative endeavours, maintains or restores order and harmony and is particularly suitable for the following utilisations:

- Creating upon the existing creation within a certain structure or form
- Expanding consciousness (within certain boundaries)
- Maintaining or restoring divine order, harmony and peace within you as well as in situations and places
- Neutralising electronic smog and pollution
- Enhancing the quality of water and food

## Experience the Seed of Life and the (bounded) Flower of Life

Return to your zero-point in the middle of your heart chakra and invite a golden Seed of Life into that chakra. Imagine the Seed of Life slowly evolving into a golden Flower of Life. Relax into your zero-point. See, sense or feel how the centre of this Flower of Life expands from your heart chakra into every cell of your body. Can you feel harmony and expansion within you? What becomes possible in your life now?

# 4.5
# Pyramid

Figure 20: The Pyramids
of Giza in Egypt

Figure 21: "El Castillo" pyramid in
Chichén Itzá/Mexico during equinox

## Description

A pyramid consists of a square at its base and four equilateral triangles rising up to a peak. Two pyramids joined at their square bases form an octahedron (see Chapter 4.6.4).

Have you ever been inside a pyramid, climbed on top of one or walked around a pyramid site? If the answer is yes, did you feel the powerful energy the pyramids exude or the high frequencies in some of their inner chambers? The architects of the ancient pyramids had profound mathematical and astronomical knowledge: Certain geometric angles in the pyramids facilitate certain high vibrations, and the exact positioning of pyramids allows for energetically powerful astronomical phenomena – often during solstices and equinoxes.

Wise ancient civilisations constructed pyramids around the world. The Pyramids of Giza (see Figure 20), for instance, are aligned with the Orion Belt. Humanity is still uncertain about their true purpose or what they were really used for. Were they energy generating and/ or energy transforming devices? For example, the Bosnian Pyramid of the Sun – in conjunction with an iron plate deep underneath it – generates a pure measurable energy beam streaming out of its top into the universe. Were the pyramids portals to the stars? Are (some of) the pyramids energetic octahedrons with their other halves residing inside the Earth, maybe in another dimension?

I love visiting pyramids and have been to sites in Egypt, Mexico, Central America, Tenerife and Bosnia-Herzegovina. I visited the main pyramid in Chichén Itzá ("El Castillo", see Figure 21) in Mexico during the September equinox of 2019. Can you see the light image of a serpent (deity) crawling down the stairs on the very left of the pyramid in Figure 21? I certainly felt a huge inflow of uplifting energy in my body and energetic system as I witnessed this one-hour light and shade phenomenon in 2019.

**Energetic qualities**

The pyramid's energetic qualities can be defined as follows:

- Energy storing device
- Energy generating device
- Energy amplification device
- Energy transforming device
- Protection of form and the human body
- Orientation and connection to the Sun and stars above or – if the peak faces downwards – the Earth below; in the case of two pyramids forming an octahedron: orientation and connection to the Sun and stars above AND the Earth below

**Utilisations**

The pyramid stores, generates and amplifies energy and raises energy levels and vibrations. It is particularly suitable for the following utilisations:

- Storing energy in a body or form
- Generating and amplifying energy (levels)
- Improving the energy flows within the body and energetic system
- Increasing the vibration of the body and energetic system
- Protecting the energy system and the energetic space around you

- Strengthening the connection to the Sun and the stars or – if the peak faces downwards – to the Earth
- In the case of two pyramids forming an octahedron: see utilisations of the octahedron in Chapter 4.6.4

Since our human systems are strongly attuned to the energy contained in pyramids, pyramid energy helps us increase our energy levels and the vibration of our energetic systems and improve the energy flows within. This leads to reduced stress, regeneration, increased vitality and a better physical, emotional and mental balance.

**Difference between a pyramid and a tetrahedron**

The geometric difference between a pyramid and a tetrahedron (see Chapter 4.6.3) lies in the base and the number of triangles rising up to the peak: The pyramid's base consists of a square with four upward rising triangles whereas the tetrahedron's base consists of a triangle with three upward rising triangles.

The pyramid and the tetrahedron share some qualities such as their orientation towards the peak. The pyramid contains both the fire element (rising peak) and the earth element (cubical base). Its base is wide and connected to the earth element – comparable to the big, extensive root system of a tree just below the surface, which allows the tree to ground and grow upwards. The tetrahedron, however, carries more fiery energy and is more action-driven.

**Experience the pyramid**

First, go into your zero-point and then see, sense or feel a huge golden pyramid in front of you. Set the intention to energetically step into the pyramid and relax into its golden frequency. Invite the pyramid's golden energy to flow into every cell of your body with the intention of increasing your energy levels. Do you feel energised and uplifted?

# 4.6
# Platonic Solids

Figure 22: Platonic solids

## Overview of the five Platonic solids

The five Platonic solids were named after the Greek philosopher Plato (427-347 BC) and Figure 22 shows crystal representations of them. The names of the Platonic solids are derived from the Greek language and indicate the number of their respective areas. From left to right starting at the upper left corner, they are:

Hexahedron – six squares
Icosahedron – twenty triangles
Tetrahedron – four triangles
Octahedron – eight triangles
Dodecahedron – twelve pentagons

The plurals of hexahedron, icosahedron, tetrahedron, octahedron and dodecahedron are hexahedrons, icosahedrons, tetrahedrons, octahedrons and dodecahedrons or hexahedra, icosahedra, tetrahedra, octahedra and dodecahedra. In this book I have opted for the first version.

The Platonic solids contain absolute symmetry and can be infinitely reproduced inside and outside through the lines inherent to them.

Each Platonic solid expresses light codes uniquely from a certain perspective and can be related to a chakra and an element (see overview table, Figure 12).

According to Plato, original wisdom can only come from an eternal field covering the whole of creation, which the soul can access. In his opinion, geometric shapes and forms are the measure of this creation. In his oeuvre "Timaeus" he describes a universal cosmology based on sacred geometry shapes and forms, which are all connected with each other. The Platonic solids themselves are probably much older than Plato as there are signs they formed part of the teachings in ancient mystery schools such as in Lemuria, Atlantis, Egypt and ancient cultures of Latin America.

# 4.6.1
# Hexahedron

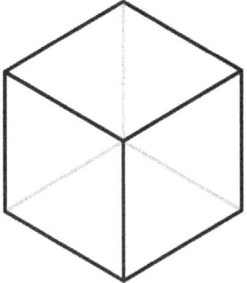

Figure 23: Hexahedron

## Description

The hexahedron – also known as the cube – consists of 6 squared areas, 8 corners and 12 edges (see Figure 23). "Hexa" is related to the word "six" in Greek. The hexagonal structure is very efficient as it leaves no wasted space when filling a plane with units of equal size as can be witnessed in bees' honeycombs. The hexahedron is related to the element of earth, the root chakra and the physical body. The highest vibration of earth is the crystalline structure.

## Energetic qualities

Its energetic qualities can be defined as follows:

- Solid, compact
- Heavy
- Restricted, tight
- Protective
- Assertive
- Form giving
- Present

## Utilisations

The solid and form-giving hexahedron is particularly suitable for the following utilisations:

- Providing stability, foundation, structure
- Grounding, connecting to the physical body and to Earth
- Protection
- Concentration and storage of energy
- Bringing light into form, materialising
- Stillness, presence

## Experience the hexahedron

Start by going into your zero-point. See, sense or feel a huge hexahedron in front of you, and by intention go into its centre. Breathe. Connect to your root chakra at the base of your spine. Invite the hexahedron to support you in grounding your physical body and connecting to Earth. Relax into its solid protective form. Do you feel more stable and grounded now?

## 4.6.2
## Icosahedron

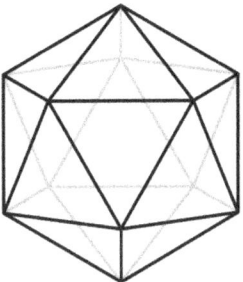

Figure 24: Icosahedron

### Description

The icosahedron – from the Greek word "ikosa" meaning "twenty" – consists of 20 equilateral triangles with 12 corners and 30 edges (see Figure 24). It is related to the element of water, the sacral chakra and emotions.

### Energetic qualities

Its energetic qualities can be defined as follows:

- Light (in weight)
- Lightful, transparent, crystalline
- Wavy, prone to movements
- Multi-faceted
- Connective, with many contact points to the outside world
- Insightful
- Combining and thus extenuating polarities, fusion between female (round, smooth) and male (edged) energies

## Utilisations

The icosahedron is a very helpful Platonic solid in times of emotional turbulence as it balances emotions, supports trust in life and brings flow to the body and energy system. It is particularly suitable for the following utilisations:

- Balancing emotions, transmuting emotional pain
- Supporting the flow of energy, unravelling stuck energies and letting go of the old
- Raising your trust
- Finding new insights and solutions, experiencing renewal and regeneration
- Starting and strengthening loving connections with the outside world

## Experience the icosahedron

Return to your zero-point and breathe. Imagine you can see, sense or feel an icosahedron right in front of you – one large enough for you to step into – and set the intention to step into its centre. You might wish to connect to the sacral chakra just below your navel, feeling any emotions which are currently present. Invite the icosahedron into your emotions and energetic system, asking it to activate itself and rotate within and around you with the intention of transmuting emotional pain and balancing your emotions. Relax, breathe deeply and feel the energies. Are you feeling more emotionally balanced now?

# 4.6.3
# Tetrahedron

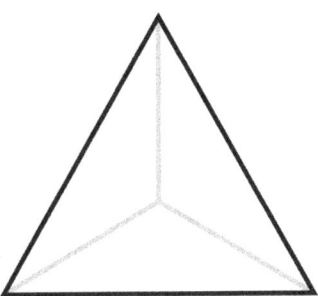

Figure 25: Tetrahedron

## Description

The tetrahedron consists of 4 equilateral triangles with 4 corners and 6 edges (see Figure 25). The word "tetrahedron" comes from the Greek word "tetra", meaning four, and this form is a basic element of creation. In fact, the tetrahedron is the first and simplest regular convex polyhedron. Water molecules and the carbon atoms within the human body display tetrahedral forms. The tetrahedron is related to the element of fire, the solar plexus chakra and the energy levels in the body.

## Energetic qualities

Its energetic qualities can be defined as follows:

- Pointed, sharp
- Fiery, electric
- Aggressive, choleric
- Aspiring, goal-oriented
- Displaying drive, determination and power of action
- Pushing forward into new areas

## Utilisations

The tetrahedron brings fiery energy to the body and energy system. It is particularly suitable for the following utilisations:

- Restoring physical balance
- Boosting your immune system, metabolism and digestion
- Activating and enhancing your sexuality
- Burning and transforming energies, for example burning off blockages and energetic connections that no longer serve you
- Activating your light body and raising your energy levels
- Raising your (masculine) energy, inducing power of action

## Sun and Earth tetrahedrons

A tetrahedron is called a Sun tetrahedron when its peak points upwards towards the Sun. This is a masculine structure associated with the following attributes: warmth, light, strength, clarity, focus, action-oriented, rotating forwards or to the right.

A tetrahedron is called an Earth tetrahedron when its peak points downwards towards the Earth. This is a feminine structure associated with the following attributes: centred in oneself, downward-pulling power, calm, heavy, connection to Earth, receiving strength and nourishment from Earth, passive-receptive, rotating backwards or to the left.

A Merkaba or star tetrahedron consists of interlocking Sun and Earth tetrahedrons.

## Experience the tetrahedron

After going into your zero-point, connect to your solar plexus chakra located at your upper abdomen and invite a tetrahedron into your body and energy system. Ask it to activate itself and support you in raising your energy levels. Feel, sense or see how the tetrahedron rotates within you. Relax and breathe. What difference did you notice?

# 4.6.4
# Octahedron

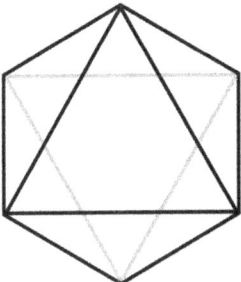

Figure 26: Octahedron

## Description

The octahedron (see Figure 26) consists of 8 equilateral triangles, 6 corners and 12 edges. In the Greek language, "okta" means "eight". The symmetrical octahedron is a combination of two pyramids connecting at their square bases. The rhombus and the diamond (see Chapter 4.10) are specific types of octahedrons. The octahedron is related to the element of air, the heart chakra and the mind.

## Energetic qualities

Its energetic qualities can be defined as follows:

- Whirling, twirling, spinning
- Dynamic, rotating fast, swirling up dust
- Focus, clarity, new horizons and visions
- Playful
- Bringing in fresh air, inspiring, innovative, energising
- Connection to the above and the below
- Two pyramids, one above and one below the ground (iceberg principle): unveiling anything hidden

## Utilisations

The octahedron brings an airy, breezy energy to your body and energy system and is particularly suitable for the following utilisations:

- Clearing and deleting blockages as well as old mental programmes and patterns
- Strengthening your mental energy, clarity and focus
- Clearing your mind and opening you to your heart's wisdom, going from your mind to your heart
- Promoting ease, joy and playfulness
- Finding new horizons and solutions on other levels, connecting to higher wisdom
- Clearing and energising places and collective fields

## Experience the octahedron

Going into your zero-point, breathe into your heart chakra and (by intention) connect to your mind. Ask yourself: Which outdated concepts, beliefs and mental patterns are ready to leave? Invite the octahedron into your mind and energetic system to set the winds of change in motion, transmuting the outdated concepts and beliefs into mental patterns that serve you. See, sense or feel how the octahedron spins and whirls around. Then tune in: What are your heart's desires and truths?

# 4.6.5
# Dodecahedron

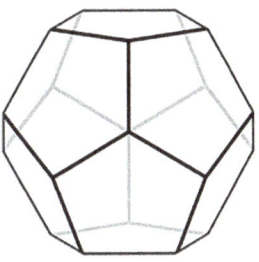

Figure 27: Dodecahedron

Figure 28: Fractal pattern:
Pentagons and Pentagrams

## Description

My favourite Platonic solid is the dodecahedron (see Figure 27) as it is a sacred form that brings in grace and universal love. In the Greek language, "dodeka" means "twelve", and the dodecahedron consists of 12 pentagons as well as 20 corners and 30 edges. Notice the fractal pattern of this form (see Figure 28): Each pentagon of the dodecahedron contains the pentagram (from a Greek word meaning "five lines"), also called the 5-pointed star (see Chapter 5.1). Inside the pentagram, there is a pentagon and inside that is another pentagram. This process continues endlessly and all the shapes exhibit the golden ratio $\varphi = a/b = b/c = 1.61803...$

The dodecahedron is related to the element of ether, the throat chakra and consciousness.

## Energetic qualities

Its energetic qualities can be defined as follows:

- Etheric
- Light (in weight)

- Lightful, transparent, like a beacon of light
- Warm
- Radiating compassion and universal love
- Expansive, going beyond blockages and frontiers
- Connecting to all of creation, embodying life force
- Inducing visions and a holistic perspective, reflecting inner wisdom and sacredness

## Utilisations

The dodecahedron connects to the Creator within and is particularly suitable for the following utilisations:

- Connection to higher guidance and unity consciousness
- Listening to inner wisdom, receiving insights, unfolding of soul plan
- Opening your heart and cells to receive grace and universal love
- Expressing your essence and the love that you are
- Stillness, presence
- Activating multidimensional abilities
- Ecstasy, life force
- Setting-up and energising a space with the heart frequency, compassion and love
- Strengthening divine order

## Experience the dodecahedron

Go into your zero-point in the middle of your heart chakra. Breathe into your throat chakra and (by intention) connect to Consciousness. Tune in: What are your soul's priorities? Which inner wisdoms and truths want to be expressed through you? Invite the dodecahedron into your energetic system with the intention of bringing in universal love and grace. See, sense or feel how the dodecahedron rotates within you and shares its gifts. Then ask yourself: "How can I share my love?"

## 4.7
## Merkaba – a Star Tetrahedron

Figure 29: Merkaba

## Description

A Merkaba – also known as a star tetrahedron – consists of two interlocking tetrahedrons of equal size, one pointing upwards, representing the Sun tetrahedron and masculine energy, and one pointing downwards, representing the Earth tetrahedron and feminine energy (see Figure 29). The word "tetrahedron" comes from the Greek word "tetra", meaning "four", and this form consists of 4 equilateral triangles. The tetrahedron has 4 corners and 6 edges and it is a basic element of creation (see Chapter 4.6.3). The two tetrahedrons of the Merkaba display different polarities and different directions of rotation. Altogether, the three-dimensional Merkaba has eight points and looks like a star (see Chapter 5.4 on the 8-pointed star).

The Ancient Egyptian word "MERKABA" reflects the trinity within us, the union of the three following elements: "MER" meaning "(Universal) Light", "KA" referring to the etheric body of a person, a vessel for the life force animating the physical body, and "BA" to that person's soul. The invisible rotating electromagnetic field of light in and around us (representing universal light, MER), the Earth tetrahedron (representing the etheric body, KA) and the Sun tetrahedron (representing the soul, BA) form the three aspects of the MER-KA-BA trinity.

The Merkaba is often referred to as our "light body", a crystalline energy structure that is both within and around us, and is related to the element of light. If you wanted to relate the Merkaba to a specific chakra, the third eye chakra in the centre of the eyebrows would feel most appropriate to me.

The Merkaba is a wonderful geometric form to harmonise polarities within you and to raise your life force and vibration. When the Merkaba is fully activated, it serves as a vehicle facilitating light body travel to other planes of existence and realities. Interestingly, according to ancient scriptures, "Merkaba" is a Hebrew word for chariot.

**Energetic qualities**

The energetic qualities of the Merkaba can be defined as follows:

- Etheric, lightful
- Energising and harmonising energy fields and the body
- Expansion beyond limitations, limitlessness
- Connection, contact, joining
- Alignment with the divine blueprint, coming into your centre
- Protection and facilitation of light body travels to other dimensions and realities

**Utilisations**

The Merkaba is particularly suitable for the following utilisations connected to the light body:

- Activation and expansion of the light body and light body consciousness
- Raising your energy levels, life force and vibration

- Harmonisation of polarities and different layers of your energetic system
- Deleting old information and programmes; programming the Merkaba/light body with new information such as the heart's desires
- Clearing and redefining contacts with the outside world
- Strengthening the connection to, and alignment with, the Earth, the Sun and universal light
- Etheric vehicle for light body travel to higher dimensions and parallel realities and planes of existence

The focus of meditating or engaging with the Merkaba has shifted in recent years. We are now letting go of the remaining old energies and paradigms. I feel the time has come to unite and merge the three aspects of our trinity – the Universal Light or Source, the (etheric) body and soul – to bring about a free human being in his or her luminous state.

**Experience the Merkaba - build your personal Merkaba field and activate it**

An easy way to build a physical (two-dimensional) personal Merkaba is to use 6 threads, each the length of your height from head to toe, and form two interlocking equilateral triangles – in the form of a 6-pointed star (see Chapter 5.2) – on the ground. Instead of a physical Merkaba, you can also build your personal Merkaba energetically through intention and by seeing it in your mind's eye.

Go into your zero-point in the middle of your heart chakra. Step into the centre of your physical personal Merkaba, or set the intention to build your personal Merkaba field around you. Feel its energy and vibration. Focus on the living intelligent light field in and around you. See, sense or feel the Earth tetrahedron that grounds you and see, sense or feel the Sun tetrahedron that connects you to the universe. See, sense or feel how both poles come together as one in your torso and how you become aligned with the Earth and the Sun at the same time. From your zero-point connect with your Merkaba through your breath. Experience your connection to yourself and to ALL THAT IS. Breathe deeply with the intention of expanding and experiencing your light body. Your Merkaba is now activated.

# 4.8
# Cosmic Egg – a Combination of the Five Platonic Solids and the Merkaba

Figure 30: Cosmic Egg

## Description

The Cosmic Egg (see Figure 30) is a beautiful and powerful sacred geometry form that combines all five Platonic solids (hexahedron, icosahedron, tetrahedron, octahedron and dodecahedron) as well as the Merkaba in one form. The octahedron is located in the centre of the Cosmic Egg. There are also two huge interlocking tetrahedrons, one pointing upwards and one pointing downwards in the form of a Merkaba. All the components of the dodecahedron fit on the outside of the hexahedron. The sharp outer points of the Cosmic Egg form part of the icosahedron, which intertwines with the dodecahedron in a golden ratio relationship. If you take one particular perspective focusing on the centre of the Cosmic Egg, all geometries come together in one balanced geometric form.

The Cosmic Egg is related to all the elements – earth, water, fire, air, ether and light – as well as to the element of your essence. If you wanted to relate it to a specific chakra, the crown chakra would feel most appropriate to me.

The Cosmic Egg has been produced anew from 2018 onwards by its manufacturers, Gregory and Gail Hail, to support you in these transformative times in taking a fresh look at your life and engaging with a new evolutionary cycle. It is a high vibrational piece constructed in alignment with your DNA pattern and the fractal progression of the universe.[18]

I love playing with the Cosmic Egg for almost any topic and find it very powerful and beautiful. Since the Cosmic Egg contains all five Platonic solids and the Merkaba, it addresses any kind of imbalance on all levels. Like an egg it facilitates the hatching of something new. To me it feels like the hatching of a golden planet – New Earth!

**Energetic qualities**

Its energetic qualities can be defined as follows:

- Golden, lightful
- Very spacious, expansive, going deep into the universe
- Containing life force
- Complete, whole
- Reflecting the original blueprint of creation
- Transcending matter while containing matter, being matter and the creator of matter at the same time (similar to the sphere)

**Utilisations**

The Cosmic Egg is particularly suitable for the following utilisations:

- Combining all the properties and effects of the Platonic solids and the Merkaba for your intention; when focusing on one Platonic

---

[18] The manufacturers of the Cosmic Egg explain its elements and properties in a video on their website (scroll down to the Cosmic Egg): http://iconnect2all.com/products/metaforms/

solid with its qualities and effects, the other four Platonic solids and the Merkaba support the process

- Transforming many levels at the same time, freeing you of limitations
- Completing, hatching, rebirthing
- Connecting to your Higher Self and to higher realms and raising your consciousness in a heartfelt and transcendent way
- Evolving relationships in your life
- Stimulating deep creativity and access to manifestation, embodying creator consciousness
- Restoring harmony and well-being on many levels
- Supporting the expansion of the consciousness of humanity and Earth

**Experience the Cosmic Egg**

Once again, go into your zero-point in the middle of your heart chakra. Connect to your crown chakra on top of your head and feel your essence. Tune in: Which aspects of your life need transformation? Which vision is ready to be birthed? What is the new life that wants to be hatched? Invite the Cosmic Egg into your body and energetic system, asking it to activate itself and to support you with this transformation and rebirth. Breathe deeply. Do you feel any sensations or shifts?

# 4.9
# Metatron's Cube

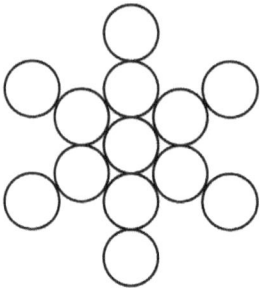

Figure 31: Fruit of Life

Figure 32: Metatron's Cube

## Description

The symbol called Fruit of Life (see Figure 31) forms the basis for Metatron's Cube. It consists of 13 (12+1) circles (or spheres) with one central circle (or sphere), an inner ring of six circles (or spheres) around the centre and an outer ring of six circles (or spheres) elongating the respective inner circles (or spheres).

Metatron's Cube is a kaleidoscope of creation (see Figure 32). It is based on the Fruit of Life (see Figure 31) and the Flower of Life (see Figure 19), and all five Platonic solids and the Merkaba can be derived from it. Connecting the centres of the inner circles with the very centre leads to the formation of a cube. Another bigger cube reveals itself when connecting the centres of the outer circles with the centre.

Metatron's Cube is connected to your soul, your soul path and to living your calling, and it is related to all the elements. If you wanted to relate it to a specific chakra, the planetary/soul (star) chakra above the crown feels most appropriate to me.

The numerology (13 = 12+1) in Metatron's Cube is worth mentioning: 12 circles gather around a central circle (or sphere(s) in a three-dimensional representation). I'd like to suggest the following interpretations: When all of your 12 multidimensional DNA strands are activated, you are catapulted into a higher dimension of consciousness. When you play all 12 musical notes consecutively, you reach a new octave of higher frequencies. The 13th circle that emerges in the centre of the other 12 circles of Metatron's Cube represents a fully conscious human being who embodies his or her innate abilities and light. From that perspective you radiate your divine nature out into the world. This has the following cause and effects: You feel the love for yourself (central circle) that leads to loving your life and the people around you (inner ring of circles) and, ultimately, to loving humanity and the world at large (outer ring of circles).

Occasionally, I've also been called to use Metatron's Cube as a basis for new sacred geometry shapes and forms. Some foster the inner qualities within us required for this new era of consciousness, others reflecting the frequencies of the new corresponding outer structures and paradigms in this world. My third book will give further information on these combinations of sacred geometry shapes and forms and, for an introduction, please see Chapter 12.

**Energetic qualities**

The energetic qualities of Metatron's Cube can be defined as follows:

- Stability, solidity
- Security, safety, protection
- Clarity, certainty, focus, insights into your soul's path
- Sense of order, structure, accomplishment of tasks
- Bringing into form, creation, manifestation of higher purpose
- Anchoring, grounding, producing tangible impacts

## Utilisations

The Fruit of Life provides the underlying structure for bearing the fruits of creation. Metatron's Cube brings stability, clarity and structure to your energy system and is particularly suitable for the following utilisations:

- Stability, safety and strength in difficult situations
- Energetic protection
- Strengthening your focus and clarity; receiving insights, particularly in connection with your higher purpose and the next steps to take
- Strengthening harmony, inner and outer balance and the experience of divine order
- Manifestation, bringing visions into form and to Earth in alignment with your soul plan/higher purpose
- Anchoring ideas and new ways of being, thus paving a way for the collective

## Variations in the use of Metatron's Cube

- Combining the circles with colours, for instance, using the colours representing the seven chakras inside the human body in the inner and central circles (6+1), or using colours for the twelve chakras inside and outside of the human body in the inner and outer circles and filling the central circle with an iridescent white light for the 13<sup>th</sup> chakra
- Combining the circles with numbers, e.g. with the Fibonacci sequence
- Meditating with Metatron's Cube, inviting it to activate itself, move and rotate within and around you and noticing if any one of its inherent forms present for you (for instance the Merkaba, the cube or any other Platonic solid)

**Experience Metatron's Cube**

Go into your zero-point. See, sense or feel a huge Metatron's Cube in front of you. Step into its centre by intention. Ask for the activation of Metatron's Cube and invite it into your energetic system with the intention of strengthening your focus and clarity about your soul plan. Tune in from your zero-point: What wants to be revealed to you right now?

# 4.10
# Diamond and Rhombus

Figure 33: Two Rhombuses

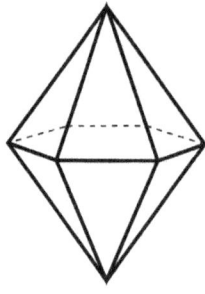

Figure 34: Diamond

## Description

A rhombus (see Figure 33) is a four-sided geometric shape, a so-called parallelogram with parallel opposite sides and equal opposite angles. A diamond (see Figure 34) is a special kind of rhombus with superb crystalline qualities. It reflects the light in all its facets – in all the rainbow colours and in a colour spectrum that is beyond what is visible with the human eye. A natural diamond crystal is an octahedron and spins as such.

The diamond can be related to your multidimensional nature and the galactic chakra above the crown.

### Energetic qualities

The energetic qualities of the diamond – and to a certain extent of the rhombus in general – can be defined as follows:

- Crystalline
- Reflector, mirror
- Accelerator, amplifier, conductor
- Antenna into galactic and angelic realms
- Activator of multidimensional facets and DNA abilities

## Utilisations

The diamond – and to a certain extent the rhombus in general – act like a mirror: You see yourself in another. The diamond also reflects the light and activates your multidimensional facets and abilities. It is particularly suitable for the following utilisations:

- Becoming aware of your different facets and reflections in the outer world, which you can then – through inner adjustments – consciously change into what you want to see
- Becoming aware of the collective nature of humanity, as it's reflected back to you
- Accelerating and magnifying the impact of your thoughts, words, emotions, actions and vibrations
- Connecting with the stars, galactic and angelic realms and building bridges to other worlds and dimensions
- Activating the multidimensional facets and abilities of your DNA such as clairvoyance and telepathic communication

## Experience the diamond

Return, once again, to your zero-point. By intention see, sense or feel yourself inside a huge diamond. The crystalline qualities of the diamond reflect the light spectrum of the galaxies. Ask the diamond to activate itself and spin around and through you while activating the multidimensional abilities of your DNA. Tune in: Which star system or realm do you feel drawn to?

# 4.11
# Infinity Symbol/Lemniscate

Figure 35: Horizontal infinity symbol

Figure 36: Vertical infinity symbol

## Description

The infinity symbol, also called "lemniscate", is well known and present in everyday life. I love it because it's both simple and profound. Consisting of two equal loops that intersect with one another in the centre, in the place of the zero-point, it's usually drawn horizontally (see Figure 35); in its upright or vertical representation, it looks like the figure "8" (see Figure 36).

The infinity symbol is connected to your infinite nature and the universal chakra way above your crown.

### Energetic qualities

The energetic qualities of the infinity symbol can be defined as follows:

*   Balance of opposites
*   Full-circling experiences, completion, integration, new beginnings
*   Infinity

- Eternity
- Universality, oneness

## Utilisations

The infinity symbol balances opposites, full-circles experiences and supports you in experiencing oneness within yourself and your surroundings. It is particularly suitable for:

- Synchronising the left and right hemispheres of your brain
- Balancing opposites, e.g. the left and right parts of the body or your feminine and masculine aspects
- Cutting cords and energies with the old (people, situations, belief systems, patterns and paradigms)
- Full-circling, completing and integrating your experiences as well as gathering your fragmented aspects
- Activating and relaxing into your infinite, eternal nature and creating anew from that expansive state of oneness

I use the horizontal infinity symbol ($\infty$) for the planetary level (Earth) and the vertical version (Figure "8") for the universal level.

## The Spirit of Ayni

The infinity symbol reflects the Law of Reciprocity, the giving and receiving from the heart. The Spirit of Ayni practiced by the Andean people is a good example of this. It implies sharing so that everyone has what he or she needs in that moment. It is about lifting each other up to higher levels through a flow of generosity and appreciation for each other and Mother Earth that can be compared to the eternal flow of the infinity symbol. The flow keeps going back and forth until it comes to balance and to full circle, remaining in the centre, in the zero-point.

## Evolution of the experience of human consciousness

To me, the infinity symbol reflects the way forward in the evolution of our experience of human consciousness. From the moment of creation, humanity went first into the experience of duality and remained there for some time. In duality, you experience yourself in and through the other person or the outer world until you "wake up" in the middle of duality to experience yourself through your infinite True Self in a state of oneness.

I feel the time has come for humanity to step out of duality into oneness as a conscious experience. It is a shift in perspective from separation with a focus on the outer world to the interconnectedness and oneness of all beings and ALL THAT IS with a focus on the inner world. It is a merging of the two polarities, the masculine and the feminine, the human self/personality and the infinite eternal self, inside you.

The infinity symbol's intersection of the two loops represents the experience of an infinite eternal state of consciousness. You experience infinity when you are out of space and time, in your physical, emotional, mental and energetic experience of the present moment. The time has come to consciously live from that zero-point. In that state, all levels of multidimensionality co-exist with each other in the present moment. You EXPERIENCE "BEING in the HERE and NOW" beyond THINKING of "NOW" as a mental concept. You are no longer identified with, nor affected by, the outer world. You are open for painting on a blank canvas.

**The evolution of the experience of human consciousness depicted in symbols**

**On a planetary level (Earth):**

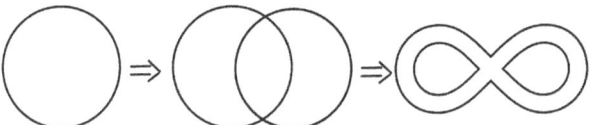

**Creation =>   Duality =>   Infinity/Oneness**

Figure 37: Evolution of the experience of human
consciousness on Earth depicted by symbols

**On the universal level:**

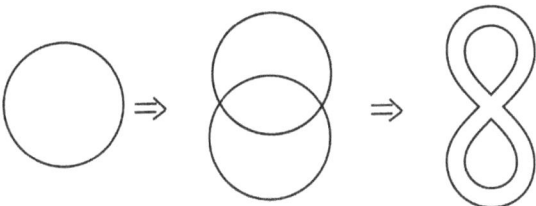

**Creation =>   Duality =>   Infinity/Oneness**

Figure 38: Evolution of the experience of human
consciousness in the universe depicted by symbols

**Experience the infinity symbol – Are you ready to full-circle the old and step into the new?**

Go into your zero-point and breathe. See, sense or feel an infinity symbol in front of you – like the number "8". You might want to draw or create a physical vertical infinity symbol (8) on the ground in front of you. Step into its centre, the intersection of the two loops, physically or energetically, and look ahead of you.

Set the intention to energetically place all the old patterns and energies that are not yours and/or no longer serve you from your energetic system into the loop behind you. Place your heart's desires and projects as fresh energies into the loop in front of you. From your present place in the centre, imagine or feel the old energies behind you and the new energies in front of you. Breathe.

When you feel the moment has come, declare that you are ready to full-circle the old and step into the new. Then step into the loop ahead of you into new beginnings. Ask your soul to cut off the loop behind you. See, sense or feel how that loop dissolves until all that is left is you inside the circle of new beginnings. Enjoy your new life!

## 4.12
## Unbounded Flower of Life

Figure 39: Unbounded Flower of Life

## Description

The Flower of Life constitutes the underlying pattern of creation of all physical form and the foundation of all existence. Everything comes from it, and everything can be returned to it.

You mostly see the Flower of Life with two or three rings around the floral pattern (see Chapter 4.4). Let's talk about the unbounded, ever-expanding Flower of Life (see Figure 39) and its importance in these times of expanding consciousness. It feels powerful and limitless to me and talks to my soul.

I encourage you to play with the unbounded Flower of Life. You can extend the Flower of Life as far as you like, gradually opening and extending it layer after layer. Experiment with seven layers (floral patterns) of the Flower of Life and paint them in the rainbow colours of the seven main chakras in the human body. Or draw an unbounded Flower of Life where the circles have a radius of the golden ratio $\varphi = 1.61803$. What do you experience? Look at a Flower of Life from a three-dimensional or even multidimensional perspective and experience the spiralling unfolding of the flower, like the unfolding of the soul's plan in a fractal universe.

**Energetic qualities**

The energetic qualities of the unbounded Flower of Life can be defined as follows:

- Creative
- Symmetrical
- Harmonious
- Containing and spreading life force energy
- Expansive in all directions and dimensions
- Limitless

**Utilisations**

The unbounded Flower of Life supports you in creating and expanding without limits in divine order and harmony and is particularly suitable for the following utilisations:

- Creating upon creation
- Maintaining or restoring divine order, harmony and peace within you, as well as in situations and places
- Neutralising harmful effects, enhancing the quality of water and foods
- Expanding consciousness across dimensions and realities
- Experiencing and living in oneness
- Facilitating the remembrance of, and the return to, the divine blueprint

**Differences in the energetic qualities and purposes of the bounded and the unbounded Flower of Life from my experience and insights**

The bounded Flower of Life with 2-3 circles (or spheres) around the floral pattern (see Chapter 4.4) represents creation within a certain structure or form (e.g. our human body). When I tune into the bounded version of the Flower of Life, I feel divinity contained in a body on planet Earth or in a similar structure.

The unbounded Flower of Life expands forward and out from its centre – just like the universe. There are no barriers, boundaries or filters. This Flower of Life is open and ever expanding in all directions and dimensions in symmetry and harmony with life, reflecting divinity, consciousness and creation. If relating it to a chakra, the divine (gateway) chakra would seem the most appropriate.

When tuning into the unbounded version of the Flower of Life, the right hemisphere of my brain is activated and my heart beats faster. My consciousness expands while I experience a gradual dissolving of my physical body and a more direct connection with infinity. The energy shifts I experience in my body feel stronger and more powerful than when engaging with the bounded Flower of Life.

The bounded Flower of Life serves its purpose of order and harmony within a certain container. However, a closed structure implies that if someone takes something from it, there is less for the rest of the group. This paradigm has so far been playing out in relationships and socio-economic and political structures and systems across the world.

I invite you to see, feel and experience the Flower of Life as limitless and multidimensional. This version of the Flower of Life supports the expansion of consciousness beyond your physical body, rational mind and emotions as well as beyond the existing paradigms and socio-economic and political structures. It activates your multidimensional and infinite nature, facilitating a new awareness and paradigm shifts.

**Experience the unbounded Flower of Life**

Returning once again to the zero-point in the middle of your heart chakra, ask for a huge multidimensional unbounded Flower of Life to emerge around you with its innermost sphere located in the middle of your heart chakra. Ask for its activation and relax into your zero-point. Relax into the perfection of the present moment and the truth of who you are. From there see, sense or feel how the centre of the Flower of Life expands into its first ring of spheres, then into the second one and so on, continuing the expansion for as long as you wish. Do you feel your limitless nature and inherent divinity?

# 4.13
# Archimedean Solids

Figure 40: The 13 Archimedean solids and the 5 Platonic solids

Have you heard of the Archimedean solids? I only came across them about four years ago. They are not widely known, yet they offer intriguing geometric and energetic qualities.

The 13 Archimedean solids are alternations of the Platonic solids (see Figure 40). The Greek mathematician and physicist Archimedes of Syracuse (287-212 BC) was the first to enumerate them. In contrast to the 5 Platonic solids, whose surfaces only display one type of polygon (such as a square, equilateral triangle or pentagon), the surfaces of the Archimedean solids show two or more different types of regular polygons.

The Archimedean solids are derived from the Platonic solids either by truncating (cutting off corners) a Platonic solid to different degrees, by an expansion process performed on certain Platonic solids or by alternations of other Archimedean solids.

As a result, the Archimedean solids contain the polygons of various Platonic solids. They could be considered the feminine counterparts of the masculine Platonic solids. Their forms and energetic qualities reflect a transformation of the Platonic solids with their sharp vertices into more feminine, spherical geometric structures. Yet, rather than just displaying feminine qualities, the Archimedean solids seem to offer a balance of masculine and feminine geometric and energetic properties. Take the example of the truncated icosahedron with 12 pentagons and 20 hexagons: The combination of features of the icosahedron and the dodecahedron leads to a more round and spherical geometry than the original forms.

After tuning into the Archimedean solids and experimenting with them, I have come to the following preliminary conclusions:

- The energetic qualities of the Archimedean solids go beyond the combinations of the energetic qualities of the individual geometric forms they are based on (e.g. icosahedron and dodecahedron in the case of the truncated icosahedron). A third entity emerges with new energetic qualities and utilisations.
- In some of the Archimedean solids, their combinations of different types of polygons are reminiscent of the reflective light facets of the diamond. The light facet effects are enhanced when the different types of polygons associated with the solid display different colours.
- The Archimedean solids feel like an evolution of the Platonic solids. They exhibit softer, more round and thus more feminine features than the sharper, more masculine forms of the Platonic solids. They seem to contain a greater balance between the masculine and the feminine energetic attributes, facilitating profound and expansive energetic effects.
- The Archimedean solids work on many levels simultaneously in a holistic way. In general, they facilitate energetic shifts towards alignment, harmony, flow and peace.
- By approaching the form of the sphere, the Archimedean solids come closer to creation and the origin of all than their

Platonic counterparts. Rather than being completely spherical, they still display rough edges, allowing light to shine through these perceived "imperfections". Since the Archimedean solids are close to the perfection of the sphere but still somewhat "imperfect", they induce our energetic systems to strive for that spherical perfection of creation by facilitating the necessary energetic shifts.

• There are 13 Archimedean solids. The number 13 (see Chapter 4.9 on Metatron's Cube and Chapter 5.9 on the 13-pointed star) reflects the outcome of activating the abilities of the multidimensional 12-strand DNA within us, leading to a radiant and powerful human being with all innate abilities activated. I feel that the Archimedean solids offer an important key in unlocking our full human potential.

The Archimedean solids have so far received far less general interest than the Platonic solids. They will become more important in connection with the more feminine sacred geometry of New Earth characterised by a stronger prominence of the sacred feminine and a greater balance between the masculine and feminine polarities, within us and in the outer world.

In my next book, which will focus on feminine sacred geometry and the inner path to New Earth, I'll present in more detail the Archimedean solids and their energetic qualities and utilisations as well as related practices.

## 4.14
# The Egyptian Ankh – a Powerful Sacred Symbol

Figure 41: The Egyptian Ankh

**Sacred symbols**

There are many sacred symbols used across ancient and temporary cultures that have powerful energetic properties and meanings. Among them are the Ankh, the Eye of Ra and the Eye of Horus used in Ancient Egypt, the Tree of Life, the symbol of the heart and the Yin Yang symbol – as well as the Om, Sri Yantra and Viswa Vajra symbols which are frequently seen in Asia.

Considering the multitude of (sacred) symbols available, it was difficult for me to decide which ones to include. The Ankh – its shape, meaning and energetic properties – has fascinated me for some time. While writing this book, the Egyptian goddess Isis stepped forward and showed me many different qualities and energetic utilisations of the Ankh and I knew it was best to focus on the Ankh and its many facets in this book, exploring other sacred symbols in future books.

**The Egyptian Ankh**

**Description**

The symbol of the Ankh looks like a cross with an oval loop at the top (see Figure 41). The Ankh resembles a human figure, with the loop representing the head. It contains female (oval loop) and male

(T-structure) elements. The Ankh was widely used in Ancient Egypt and represents the key of (eternal) life. It acts as a tuning fork for frequencies and directs sounds.

Through this combination of female and male elements, the Ankh introduces a new quality to the standard sacred geometry shapes and forms, which usually consist of lines, edges and corners on the one hand or loops, circles and spherical structures on the other.

**Energetic qualities**

The energetic qualities of the Ankh can be defined as follows:

- Connection to the Higher Self and higher realms
- Fertility, life force
- Transformation
- Tuning fork for frequencies, directing sounds
- Key to the creation of a new reality, giving birth to something new
- Key to eternal life, opening the gates of transition to a new life

**Utilisations**

The Ankh opens the doors to your Higher Self and to (eternal) life, supporting you in giving birth to new realities. It is particularly suitable for the following utilisations:

- Connecting to your Higher Self and higher realms with their wisdom and heart-based authentic power
- Increasing your life force
- Supporting transformation and the creation of new realities
- Supporting you in choosing to be here on Earth at this time (e.g. in cases of depression or suicidal tendencies)
- Supporting loved ones on their way home into another dimension/life

## Different aspects of the Ankh

I have been shown different types of the Ankh that can be used for the following purposes:

- The Upside-Down Ankh: facilitating a deeper connection to Earth
- The Burning Ankh: destroying old energies and limitations
- The Kundalini Ankh: activating the heart chakra, life force and kundalini energy
- The Golden-White Ankh with rays of violet, gold and diamond white light: supporting transmutation, purification and activation of the essence within you
- The Illuminated Ankh: spreading grace and universal love
- The Rainbow Ankh: building bridges to other people, dimensions and star systems as well as supporting loved ones on their way into another dimension/life

Tune in to see which type of Ankh is presenting for you right now. You might also find other aspects of the Ankh to play with.

You will find the corresponding images and practices of the various Ankhs in Chapter 7.15.

## Experience the Ankh

Once again, return to your zero-point in the middle of your heart chakra. If you have a physical representation of an Ankh, you might want to hold it in your hands. Connect to a physical Ankh or visualise, sense or feel an energetic Ankh in front of you. With your intention, invite the Ankh to come into your energy system, asking it to activate itself and rotate in your energy system with the intention of increasing your life force. Breathe. Ask the rotating Ankh to expand into every cell of your body. Do you feel energised?

# 4.15
# Introduction to Spiral Patterns, Vortices and Tori

## Spiral patterns

Figure 42: Spiral fern leaf      Figure 43: Phi      Figure 44: Treble Clef

Evolution occurs in spirals and through fractals.[19] If you change anything, you change everything as anything is connected to everything else in nature and the cosmos. There are many – familiar – natural examples of spiral patterns such as the Nautilus shell, human DNA, hurricanes as well as the forms of galaxies. Plants and leaves unwind in a spiral (see spiral fern leaf in Figure 42).

The Nautilus shell (see Figure 4) resembles the Fibonacci spiral, spiralling clockwise like an expanding universe. The golden ratio with its symbol phi (see Figure 43) is somewhat visible in the treble clef (see Figure 44). The treble clef's swinging pattern reflects the soft power of sound frequency and the multidimensional vibrations inherent in music.

The spiral reflects the evolution of consciousness in an ever-expanding universe. Focusing on spirals, tracing their paths and engaging with them can catapult you into higher dimensions of consciousness, taking you on a journey into yourself (spiralling inwards) and outside of yourself (spiralling outwards). By spiralling you re-encounter familiar patterns and experiences – but this time from a higher

---

[19] Chapter 2 provides more information on the fractality of the universe.

evolutionary level. It feels like shedding layers – comparable to the serpent that repeatedly sheds its skin. You might also compare it to peeling an onion, thus going deeper to its very core.

In my experience, spiralling clockwise facilitates raising your vibration and restoring divine order and harmony whereas spiralling anti-clockwise facilitates releasing, removing something that does not belong (anymore) and transmuting the old. Clockwise spirals might also reflect the process of venturing out whereas anti-clockwise spirals might mean going deeper within. Tune in for your truth, as your experience might be different (see also my comment on the directions of rotations in Chapter 2).

Evolution happens in a multidimensional and not in a linear way. The spiralling evolution facilitates unexpected solutions and fast progress; there is no need to go linearly, in a slow step-by-step approach, from A to B; just take the fast journey upwards or inwards.

**Vortex/Vortices**

Figure 45: Vortex

Spiralling around yourself or around something in a clockwise direction creates a centrifugal power. When spiral patterns move powerfully, they create a vortex of energy. Vortices (or vortexes) are powerful and transformational energy centres. Examples of vortices are the chakras of the human body (see Figure 11).

On the physical Earth plane, you find energetic vortices in specific locations such as at sacred sites around the world where energy is either entering into the Earth or powerfully projecting out of the Earth's plane. In the cosmos, you find energetic vortices in wormholes, for example (see Figure 45).

When engaging with sacred geometry shapes and forms, you can create these vortices by intention, by asking the geometries to form a vortex or by installing a vortex of a particular shape or form in your energy system. Examples of how to work with sacred geometry vortices are found in Chapters 6 and 7.

## Torus/Tori

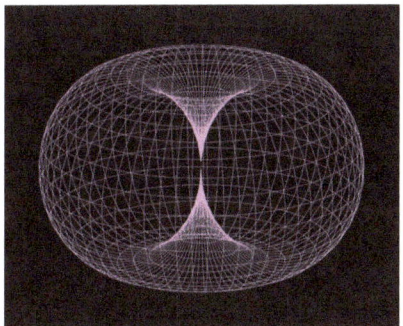

Figure 46: Torus

A torus (plural: tori) is based on a self-organising principle: The energy ventures out from its centre to come back again. Its form resembles a donut or an apple (see Figure 46). It is a perfectly balanced, dynamic energetic swirl, which harmonises and maintains the etheric energy flow between poles. It can be viewed as an implosion and creation field. The torus field is one of the most important patterns of nature. It is in all living things: in small atoms, minerals, plants and animals – even the magnetospheres of the Earth and galactic centres are toroidal. The torus distributes energies equally into all systems. It is self-preserving, maintains life flow and grants a constant energy flow on different levels.

In human beings, the torus field emerges from the centre of the heart chakra. It is a natural layer of protection, which strengthens the human organism, balances the human energy field and can be expanded through conscious deep breath. The HeartMath Institute offers information and images of the powerful toroidal electromagnetic field generated by the heart.[20]

Spiral patterns, vortices and tori are essential elements in the exploration and use of sacred geometry due to their energetic power and importance. These will be explored in more detail in my next book.

---

[20] https://www.heartmath.org/articles-of-the-heart/global-interconnectedness/each-individual-impacts-the-field-environment/

# Chapter 5

# Overview of the Stars

Figure 47: 6-pointed Sun

Figure 48: Star Anise

In this chapter we will travel to and with the stars. You find them in the heavens above (see Figure 47) and on Earth below (see Figure 48). As in the last chapter, I'll present a variety of stars with their energetic qualities and utilisations and invite you to explore their gifts through a first energetic experience. Watch out for stars in your surroundings – not only in the night sky but also during your day on Earth!

**Overview table**

The table below (see Figure 50) gives an overview of the different stars, their meanings and utilisations and where to find them. These are my experiences and contemplations:

- Single-digit stars focus on the individual or personal level of each and every one of us.
- Stars with a number of points from 10 to 19 focus on the collective level of humanity on Earth through each and every one of us.
- Stars with more than 20 points focus on collective human consciousness related to galactic and universal levels through each and every one of us.
- I feel guided to present information up to the 33-pointed star at this moment.

Since we are all fractals of the greater All, our energies, thoughts, emotions, actions and vibrations affect humanity, planetary levels and on to galactic and universal levels.

Due to their collective nature, you might not feel the energies of the stars with double-digit numbers as strongly as those with single-digit numbers. However, their energies will become more noticeable in the near future.

The stars can be drawn as standalone stars with their specific number of points (e.g. an 18-pointed star) or as two or more stars coming together as one (e.g. two 9-pointed stars or three 6-pointed stars coming together to form one 18-pointed star). Some examples are presented in the table below:

7-pointed star: standalone star
9-pointed star: three triangles coming together to form a 9-pointed star
10-pointed star: two pentagrams coming together to form a 10-pointed star

Stars may also be drawn as multidimensional layers of two or more stars of different radiuses on top of each other like the petals of a flower (e.g. an 18-pointed star drawn as two 9-pointed stars or three 6-pointed stars of different radiuses on top of each other, see Figure 49).

Figure 49: 18-pointed star composed of three layers of 6-pointed stars

Stars with double-digit numbers display similar energetic qualities and utilisations as their counterparts with single-digit numbers on a collective rather than a personal level. Example: The 7-pointed star supports you individually in aligning with natural and universal cycles and laws; the 14 (=2*7)-pointed star supports humanity with overall coherence and balance with natural and cosmic cycles on Earth through you. Due to these similarities and in order to avoid repetition or unnecessary information, I have kept the information on the stars with double-digit numbers shorter than usual and combined the energetic qualities and utilisations under one heading in the corresponding Chapters 5.6 to 5.17. The practices offered to experience the energies of the stars with double-digit numbers can be found in the appropriate context and order in Chapters 7.17, 7.18 and 7.19.

| Shape | Name | Meaning/Utilisation | Main References in Chapters |
|---|---|---|---|
|  | 5-pointed star/ Pentagram | Remembering and expressing your essence, your light and divine nature | 4.6.5; 5.1; 5.6; 7.6; 7.10 |
|  | 6-pointed star/ Star of David | Alignment with the Earth and the Sun; centring yourself; harmonisation of polarities | 5.2; 5.8; 7.13; 7.17 |
|  | 7-pointed star | Alignment with the rhythms, cycles and laws of nature and the universe; becoming natural again | 5.3; 5.10; 7.11; 7.18; 8 |
|  | 8-pointed star | Union of opposites; expansion of consciousness | 5.4; 5.12; 5.16; 7.12; 7.13; 7.19 |
|  | 9-pointed star | Completion; releasing the old; making way for new beginnings | 5.5; 5.14; 7.7; 7.19 |
|  | 10-pointed star | Unity consciousness; experiencing yourself as one with another => formation of the human collective; shift from the individual to the collective perspective | 5.6; 7.6; 7.17 |

| | | | |
|---|---|---|---|
| | 11-pointed star | First master number; new beginnings; transition from experiencing unity consciousness within you to sharing your light and gifts with the world | 5.7; 7.17 |
| | 12-pointed star | Vertical alignment and horizontal outreach: living your mastery and calling from your soul | 5.8; 5.16; 7.17; 7.18 |
| | 13-pointed star | 12+1: Activation of multidimensional DNA; entering the miracle zone; transition 12->14-pointed star | 5.9; 7.18 |
| | 14-pointed star | Overall coherence, harmony and balance with natural and cosmic cycles on Earth | 5.10; 7.18; 7.19 |
| | 15-pointed star | Transition 14->16-pointed star; transition from overall coherence and harmony to oneness | 5.11; 7.19 |
| | 16-pointed star | Experiencing oneness as a human collective | 5.12; 7.19 |

|  | 17-pointed star | Transition 16->18-pointed star; transition from oneness to stepping out of old collective paradigms | 5.13; 7.19 |
|---|---|---|---|
|  | 18-pointed star | Ending old collective paradigms; stepping out of the old "matrix", i.e. the old socio-economic and political paradigms and contexts | 5.14; 7.19 |
|  | 22-pointed star | Second master number; new beginnings on a collective level of humanity; the universe is inside you | 5.15; 7.19 |
|  | 24-pointed star | Experiencing oneness with the universe | 5.16; 7.19 |
|  | 33-pointed star | Third master number; expansion of the human collective's consciousness into galactic and universal levels; everything is possible | 5.17; 7.19 |

Figure 50: Overview of the stars and their meanings and utilisations

# 5.1
# 5-Pointed Star/Pentagram

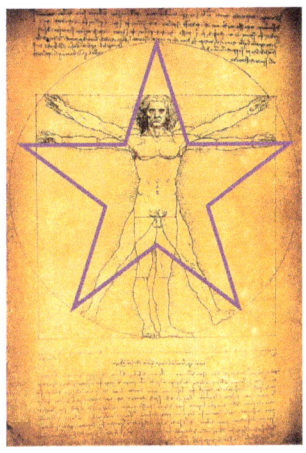

Figure 51: The Vitruvian
Man in/as a pentagram

Figure 52: 5-pointed stars
in flowers

## Description

The pentagram (from a Greek word meaning "five lines") is also known as a star with five points, and it is related to the dodecahedron with its 12 pentagons (see Chapter 4.6.5).

The human body is built according to sacred geometric proportions. When you stand straight and look forward with your arms outstretched in a horizontal line at shoulder height and your legs a little more than hip-width apart, your body forms a pentagram.

In Figure 51 you can see this pentagram depicted in artist Leonardo da Vinci's illustration of the "Vitruvian Man". The navel is in the pentagram's centre. The distance between your feet and navel divided by the distance between your navel and the top of your head approximates the golden ratio φ = 1.61803...

The pentagram is very present in nature. Look at the beautiful purple flower with a yellow 5-pointed star in its centre in Figure 52. I encourage you to start noticing 5-pointed stars in your surroundings – in flowers, fruits or vegetables, for example.

**Energetic qualities**

Its energetic qualities can be defined as follows:

- Lightful
- Joyful, playful
- Expansive
- Life force
- Sacred
- Inner wisdom, holistic perspective
- Essence
- Universal love

**Utilisations**

The pentagram connects you to your essence and divine nature and is particularly suitable for the following utilisations:

- Remembering and expressing your essence, your light and divine nature
- Opening the heart to love and vulnerability
- Letting go of self-criticism and limiting judgments about yourself
- Listening to inner wisdom, taking a holistic perspective and opening up to your soul plan
- Experiencing joy, life force, presence
- Setting-up and energising a space with the heart frequency and universal love
- Feeling the sacredness of ALL THAT IS

In view of their close connection, the energetic qualities and utilisations of the pentagram are similar to the ones of the dodecahedron. I use the pentagram for experiencing my personal essence, joy and my connection to ALL THAT IS whereas I use the dodecahedron for collective topics and bringing in universal love and grace from creation.

**Experience the 5-pointed star**

Go into your zero-point and breathe. See, sense or feel a huge 5-pointed star standing in front of you. By intention energetically step into this 5-pointed star and become the 5-pointed star like the Vitruvian (hu-)man in Figure 51. By intention activate this pentagram within you and see, sense or feel how the energy of your essence flows from your heart centre into all 5 points of the star located in your head, in your hands and in your feet.

## 5.2
## 6-Pointed Star/Star of David

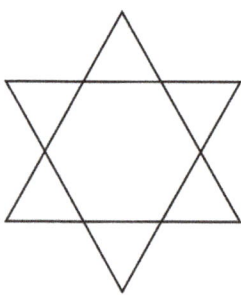

Figure 53: 6-pointed star

Figure 54: 6-pointed tulip

### Description

In its two-dimensional representation, the 6-pointed star – also known as the "Star of David" – is a combination of two equilateral triangles, one pointing upwards and one pointing downwards (see Figure 53). In a three-dimensional representation with two tetrahedrons, it turns into a Merkaba or a star tetrahedron (see Chapter 4.7).

Look out for 6-pointed stars in nature, for example in the radiating sun or an opening tulip (see Figures 47 and 54). The 6-pointed star is also visible in the centre of the six circles of the Seed of Life (see Figure 18).

### Energetic qualities

The energetic qualities of the 6-pointed star can be defined as follows:

- Etheric, lightful
- Energising
- Connection to the above and the below, to the Sun and the Earth
- Alignment, coming into your centre
- Harmonising polarities

## Utilisations

The 6-pointed star centres you, aligning you with the universe/Sun and the Earth and is particularly suitable for the following utilisations:

- Strengthening the connection to, and alignment with, the Earth and the Sun
- Coming into your centre and your zero-point
- Harmonisation of polarities and different layers of your energetic system

In view of their close connection, the energetic qualities and utilisations of the 6-pointed star are similar to the ones of the Merkaba. I use the 6-pointed star for aligning with the Earth and the Sun and centring myself whereas I use the Merkaba for activating, clearing and reprogramming my light body (consciousness) as well as for light body travel.

The 6-pointed star focuses on your vertical connection to, and expansion into, the Earth and the Sun. The 12-pointed star (see Chapter 5.8) complements this vertical connection with your horizontal connection to the world (through the additional two triangles to the left and to the right). The 12-pointed star thus symbolises the expansion of a centred and vertically aligned human being into the world at large. I use the 6-pointed star for coming into my centre, into balance and alignment with the Earth and Sun first, before continuing with the 12-pointed star to support my outreach in the world.

## Experience the 6-pointed star

Build your own personal 6-pointed star with 6 threads, each of the length of your height from head to toe, by forming two interlocking equilateral triangles on the ground. Instead of a physical version, you can also see your 6-pointed star in your mind's eye or feel or sense it energetically. Go into your zero-point. Step into the centre of your personal 6-pointed star physically or by intention and feel its energy. See, sense or feel your connection to the Earth below through the downwards-pointing triangle and breathe into it to make it stronger. See, sense or feel your connection to the Sun above through the upwards-pointing triangle and breathe into it to make it stronger. Connect to and feel into your torso and vertically align and centre yourself.

**Experience the special attributes of a crystalline snowflake**

Figure 55: Snowflake in the form of a 6-pointed star

Have you ever truly explored the nature of a snowflake? Snowflakes can take the form of a 6-pointed star (see Figure 55) with a central structure and 6 points reaching outwards, displaying a beautiful interconnection between the collective (central structure) and the individual (points). This type of crystalline structure helps to activate the crystalline nature of the physical body.

Experience the specific crystalline structure of a snowflake:

- Placing a physical form or printout of the crystalline structure of a 6-pointed star snowflake on certain body parts, especially where you feel density or uncomfortable body sensations
- Meditating with the crystalline structure of this snowflake, connecting with it, inviting it by intention into your energy field, activating it within you, then feeling or sensing the snowflake and its energetic properties

# 5.3
# 7-Pointed Star

Figure 56: Blueberry
7-pointed star

Figure 57: 7-pointed star

## Description

A 7-pointed star, also called a septagram or heptagram, forms a unity with seven points. Due to its uneven number of points (7), the star does not appear as symmetrical as its even-numbered counterparts. The 7-pointed star can have a wide inner space (see Figure 56), or more jagged points as in Figure 57. Opposite a point or a peak on one side of the star, there is an opening on the other side, displaying polarity and balance.

The 7-pointed star reflects the cyclical attributes and inherent rhythms of creation, nature and the cosmos, as well as natural and cosmic laws. The natural and cosmic cycles are, for example, apparent in the following phenomena:

- 7 days of creation
- 7 days of the week
- Recurring seasons
- Recurring musical notes
- Moon cycles
- Planetary cycles
- Ebb and flow of the oceans

The importance of the number 7 is reflected in the 7 days of creation, the 7 days of the week, the 7 main chakras of the human body and the 7 universal laws also known as the "7 Hermetic Principles", which are teachings by Thoth alias Hermes Trismegistus.

**Energetic qualities**

The energetic qualities of the 7-pointed star can be defined as follows:

- Cyclical
- Rhythmical
- Natural, innocent
- Wheel that keeps on turning
- Spiralling (in a multidimensional way)
- Alchemical

**Utilisations**

The 7-pointed star supports you in regaining balance and harmony within yourself and with your surroundings and is particularly suitable for the following utilisations:

- Connection to the Earth, nature and the cosmos
- Alignment with the rhythms, cycles and laws of nature and the cosmos
- Returning to harmony with your body and to your organic flow
- Returning to your innocence, embracing your inner child, becoming natural again
- Maintaining an ecological equilibrium, using Earth's gifts in a balanced way

**Experience the 7-pointed star**

Go into your zero-point and breathe. You might want to close your eyes. Set the intention to energetically step into a 7-pointed star that is right in front of you and see, sense or feel how it expands in all directions. Breathe into the expansion. See, sense, feel or know that you are in flow with all life and in alignment with natural cycles and rhythms. Nothing in nature questions its inherent value or purpose. Will you return to being natural?

**Two special versions of the 7-pointed star: the Fairy Star and the Hermetic Principles Star**

**The 7-pointed Fairy Star: Connection to, and alignment with, the rhythms and cycles of nature**

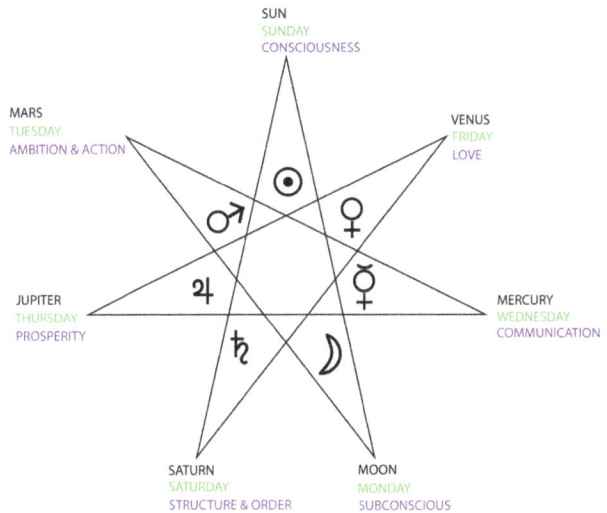

Figure 58: 7-pointed Fairy Star

The 7-pointed Fairy Star (see Figure 58) supports you in attuning to natural cycles and in living in harmony and balance on Earth. It is said to be a symbol used by fairies and elves for their purposes. The Fairy Star depicts the 7 days of the week with their cosmic connections and related topics. The 7 days of the week are not allocated next to each other. In order to proceed from one day to the next, you first move into the opposite direction from your starting point, thereby crossing the centre of the star. These movements to the opposite sides support the process of balancing and harmonising opposites.

## The 7-pointed Hermetic Principles Star: Connection to, and alignment with, the rhythms and laws of the universe

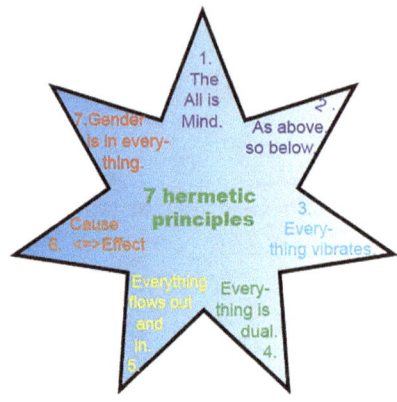

Figure 59: 7-pointed Hermetic Principles Star

The 7 Hermetic Principles are universal laws that teach us how to live in alignment and balance with the universe, cosmos and ALL THAT IS. Thoth, alias Hermes Trismegistus, showed me the 7-pointed Hermetic Principles Star (see Figure 59) in a meditation. It offers a wide perspective on the underlying mechanisms of life and assists us to flow and co-create with the universe. Through the 7 universal laws in the 7 points of the star, it is infused with insights on conscious and subconscious levels about how the universe operates.

I used the 7-pointed Hermetic Principles Star while exploring the deeper meaning and applications of the 7 universal laws from 11/2019 until 01/2020. I experimented with one Hermetic Principle per week, slowly building up the seven points of this star. During this process, I received several insights and changed certain habits that no longer served me to new, uplifting habits and I now feel more in tune with life.

In Chapter 8, I invite you to come with me on a journey exploring the foundations and principles of our universe and applying them to your life through the 7-pointed Hermetic Principles Star.

## 5.4
## 8-Pointed Star

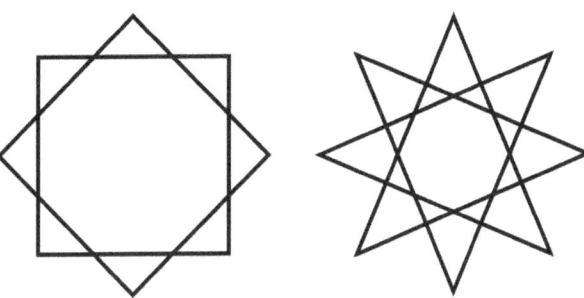

Figures 60 and 61: 8-pointed stars

## Description

There are various versions of the 8-pointed star. A popular version depicts a union or marriage of two squares, combining a square standing on its bottom line with a square standing on one corner (see Figure 60). You can also draw the 8-pointed star by joining its eight points in one go (see Figure 61). In its centre, you will find the union of the two squares of the previous figure.

A version of the 8-pointed star with protruding points on all eight sides is called a male octagon (see Figure 60). In the version of the female octagon, the same eight points are folded inwards and form recesses (see Figure 61). The hermaphrodite version has four protrusions and four recesses forming a pointed cross in a square.[21]

The 8-pointed star is related to infinity which is represented by the number "8" (see Chapter 4.11). It is a popular image of the Islamic architecture in southern Spain. In the Christian tradition, the 8-pointed star, whose name is also "Star of Bethlehem", is the

---

[21] For images of the three genders of 8-pointed stars as well as many other combinations and variations of the 8-pointed star see J. Mitchell, A. Brown: How the world is made, p. 126 ff.

foundational shape for some Christmas star ornaments used to celebrate the birth of Christ – or Christ Consciousness – on Earth. The three-dimensional Merkaba with its 8 points representing the light body (see Chapter 4.7) is another example of the importance of the 8-pointed star.

## Energetic qualities

Its energetic qualities can be defined as follows:

- Expansion, openings
- Union and marriage of two polarities (male/female, heaven/ Earth, Higher Self/human self)
- Balance, harmony and peace
- Grounding higher consciousness, birth of Christ Consciousness

## Utilisations

The expansive 8-pointed star is particularly suitable for the following utilisations:

- Expansion of consciousness
- Expansion of creativity
- Balancing, integrating and/or transcending polarities
- Grounding the expanded consciousness in the world, birth of Christ Consciousness on Earth – "love made visible"

Depending on your level of consciousness and practice, the 8-pointed star supports your expansion of consciousness until your Higher Self and human self become one. Then Christ Consciousness is born on Earth in and through you, and the perception of heaven on Earth is restored within you.

## Examples of the 8-pointed star in architecture and nature

There are a number of examples of 8-pointed stars in architecture and nature. The 8-pointed star is one of the essential elements in the Islamic tradition in Andalusia/Spain. In the old city quarters of Granada and the Alhambra Palace you will find many 8-pointed stars on pavements, walls and ceilings.

Figure 62: 8-pointed stars on a wall in the Alhambra Palace in Granada/Spain

Look at the 8-pointed star in the centre of the photo in Figure 62. It is embedded in a bigger 8-pointed star, which is in turn embedded in an even bigger 8-pointed star. The 8-pointed stars look similar but not alike. This type of fractal pattern expresses infinity through the recurrence of similar (rather than repeating) structures – a concept that has long been used in Islamic design.[22]

Another beautiful example of the 8-pointed star in a religious building is the Star of Bethlehem in the Lady Chapel of the Rosslyn Chapel in Scotland. Around the sides of that 8-pointed star, there are eight figures connected to the story of the birth of Jesus Christ (Mother Mary holding baby Jesus, the manger, the Three Magi and three shepherds).

---

[22] See Daud Sutton, Islamic Design, 2007, p. 30.

You will also find patterns of 8-pointed stars in flowers, plants and nature in general (see Figure 63).

Figure 63: 8-pointed star flower

## Experience the 8-pointed star

Build your own 8-pointed star consisting of two squares on the ground. You might want to use 8 threads, each of the length of your height from head to toe. Instead of a physical version, you can also create your 8-pointed star energetically through intention or by seeing it in your mind's eye. Go into your zero-point. Imagine a huge 8-pointed star in front of you. By intention step into its centre and experience its energy. Breathe into it to make it stronger. See, sense or feel how your energetic system expands and expands. Can you perceive your true nature?

## 5.5
## 9-Pointed Star

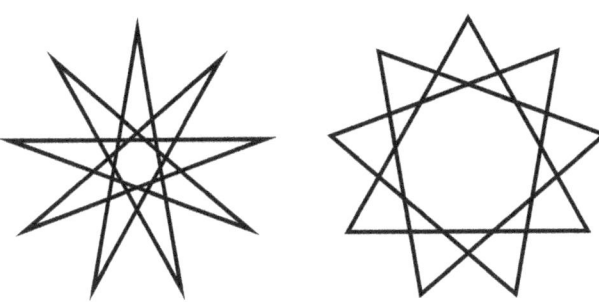

Figures 64 and 65: 9-pointed stars

## Description

A 9-pointed star can be drawn in one go, forming a unity with nine points (see Figure 64). In its centre are three interlocking equilateral triangles of equal size, representing another version of a 9-pointed star (see Figure 65). Each of the nine points faces an opening between two points (recess) on its opposite side, reflecting polarity and balance.

The numerology is important for the energetic qualities and utilisations of the 9-pointed star. The number 9 represents completion. The following number 10 with a cross total of 1 indicates a new beginning.

### Energetic qualities

The energetic qualities of the 9-pointed star can be defined as follows:

- Completion
- Perseverance (leading to completion)
- Stocktaking
- Integration, anchoring

## Utilisations

The 9-pointed star is particularly suitable for the following utilisations:

- Completing and releasing old patterns
- Smashing the old and making way for new beginnings such as demolishing walls of protection and structures you have erected which do not serve you anymore
- Integrating and anchoring your new awareness

## Experience the 9-pointed star

Go into your zero-point. Choose a pattern that no longer serves you and that you're ready to release. Alternatively, ask your soul to activate such a pattern within you. By focusing on this pattern, activate it within you by intention and see, sense or feel it in your body and energy system. Once you perceive the pattern within you, invite the 9-pointed star into your body and energy system. Ask the 9-pointed star to activate itself and to rotate and move with the intention of clearing this pattern and completing it within you. In which direction does the star rotate – clockwise or anti-clockwise? You might experience a spiralling or spinning sensation. Breathe and let the star do its work. When the work is done and the clearing completed, turn the 9-pointed star by intention in the opposite direction to the initial rotation to seal the completion. Tune in: Are you ready to step into something new?

## 5.6
## 10-Pointed Star

Figure 66: 10-pointed star

### Description

A 10-pointed star can be drawn in one go or as two interlocking pentagrams of equal size (see Figure 66).

### Energetic qualities and utilisations

The 10-pointed star can be regarded as the union of two 5-pointed stars or pentagrams (see Chapter 5.1). The energetic qualities of the 10-pointed star are very similar to the ones of the 5-pointed star – on a collective rather than an individual level. I use the 5-pointed star for remembering, activating and living my personal essence, whereas I use the 10-pointed star for experiencing my essence in conjunction with that of another person and our joint creations. The 10-pointed star is thus connected to activating and embodying unity consciousness: You in your essence (first 5-pointed star) experience yourself also through another essence (second 5-pointed star), jointly creating a 10-pointed star. The 10-pointed star supports your refinement through the interaction with others and ultimately facilitates unity consciousness. This unity consciousness comes with a shift from the individual to the collective perspective and facilitates the conscious experience of a human collective.

Please refer to Chapter 7.17 to experience the 10-pointed star.

## 5.7
## 11-Pointed Star

Figure 67: 11-pointed star

### Description

The 11-pointed star (see Figure 67) appears asymmetrical since the geometric shape of the 10-pointed star has been stirred up to find its new order and shape in the four triangles of the 12-pointed star.

The number 11 is a master number and is connected to intuition, higher wisdom and special abilities. In numerology, a pair of the same numbers is called a master number: 11, 22, 33, 44 and so on. It is not reduced any further to the cross total of a single digit number but stands in its own power. The master numbers are gateways and portals to the next evolutionary levels. The number 11 is the first master number.

### Energetic qualities and utilisations

The 11-pointed star facilitates new beginnings and marks the journey of transition from the 10-pointed star to the 12-pointed star with their respective energetic qualities and utilisations. In other words, the 11-pointed star facilitates your transition from experiencing unity consciousness internally (reflected by the 10-pointed star) to sharing your light and gifts by living your calling and expressing your mastery in the outer world (reflected by the 12-pointed star).

The 11-pointed star is a portal from the internal to the external world. It assists you in this process of getting ready to shine your light in the world.

I encourage you to play with the 11-pointed star when you are clear about your vision and what you want to offer to the world in order to assist you in taking the necessary steps.

Please refer to Chapter 7.17 to experience the 11-pointed star.

# 5.8
# 12-Pointed Star

Figure 68: 12-pointed star

## Description

The 12-pointed star is a combination of four equilateral triangles, one pointing upwards, one downwards and two triangles pointing to the left and right (see Figure 68). If you look at it from a three-dimensional perspective, you see two Merkabas with four tetrahedrons pointing upwards, downwards and to the left and right sides.

### Energetic qualities and utilisations

The upward and downward pointing triangles or tetrahedrons establish the vertical connection to the Sun – or the heavens above – and the Earth below. The two triangles or tetrahedrons pointing to the left and right ensure the horizontal connection and thus the outreach to the world at large. A 12-pointed star can be regarded as the collective version of the 6-pointed star or – in its three-dimensional representation – of a Merkaba, thus reflecting a collective light body.

The 12-pointed star activates your calling and mastery and facilitates synergies and synchronicities in this regard. A prerequisite to living mastery is being aware that you are much more than your human nature with a two-strand DNA rooted in survival. You have a multidimensional 12-strand DNA that serves as a basis for living your mastery. The 12-pointed star strengthens your purpose and impact in the world. With the help of your connection and alignment to the Earth and the heavens above, you can bring your creations into the world, affecting many more people for the highest and best good of all concerned.

Please refer to Chapter 7.17 to experience the 12-pointed star.

## 5.9
## 13-Pointed Star

Figure 69:
13-pointed star

Figure 70: Cactus with
12+1 areoles

### Description

The 13-pointed star (see Figure 69) is an expression of the important spiritual number 13, which is regarded as a doorway and portal into higher dimensions and levels of consciousness. For me, the number 13 reflects the outcome of activating the 12 strands of DNA within you, leading to a radiant and powerful human being with all innate abilities activated. This also facilitates entering the miracle zone and experiencing miracles. This cactus with 12+1 areoles caught my attention as a natural symbol and reflection of this phenomenon (see Figure 70).

### Energetic qualities and utilisations

The 13-pointed star marks the journey of transition from the 12-pointed star to the 14-pointed star with their respective energetic qualities and utilisations. In other words, the 13-pointed star facilitates the journey from living your calling and expressing your mastery (reflected by the 12-pointed star) to experiencing the reflection of your internal harmony and balance in your outer world (depicted by the 14-pointed star).

The 13-pointed star assists you in the internal process of integrating your calling and mastery through activating your multidimensional DNA and innate abilities, as well as reaching a certain level of harmony within, which is then reflected back to you.

Please refer to Chapter 7.18 to experience the 13-pointed star.

## 5.10
## 14-Pointed Star

Figure 71: 14-pointed star

### Description

The 14-pointed star can be drawn in one go or as a combination of two 7-pointed stars (see Figure 71).

### Energetic qualities and utilisations

The 7-pointed star reflects the cyclical attributes and inherent rhythms of creation, nature and the cosmos as well as natural and cosmic laws. When in harmony and equilibrium with natural and cosmic cycles and laws on an individual level, the 14-pointed star facilitates the mirror of this inner harmony in your surroundings and life. This could mean more flow and synchronicities in your life and having the "right" people and situations come to you with ease and grace.

If we continue living in harmony with natural rhythms and universal laws on an individual level, we will return to living in harmony with nature and the cosmos as a human collective. If a critical mass of humanity on Earth sees itself as part of all life and lives in harmony and balance with other beings on Earth and in the cosmos, the experience of ecological balance and overall harmony can be restored on Earth and in our universe.

Please refer to Chapter 7.18 to experience the 14-pointed star.

# 5.11
# 15-Pointed Star

Figure 72: 15-pointed star

## Description

The 15-pointed star can be drawn in one go (see Figure 72) or as a combination of three 5-pointed stars.

## Energetic qualities and utilisations

The 15-pointed star marks the journey of transition from the 14-pointed star to the 16-pointed star with their respective energetic qualities and utilisations. In other words, the 15-pointed star facilitates your transition from experiencing overall harmony and balance with natural and universal rhythms and cycles, as well as flow in your life (reflected by the 14-pointed star), to experiencing oneness or Christ Consciousness (reflected by the 16-pointed star). To me, experiencing Christ Consciousness means feeling compassion for all life, seeing the divine light in everyone and everything, thereby experiencing oneness through the True Self.

Please refer to Chapter 7.19 to experience the 15-pointed star.

## 5.12
## 16-Pointed Star

Figure 73: 16-pointed star

### Description

The 16-pointed star can be drawn in one go or as a combination of two 8-pointed stars (see Figure 73).

### Energetic qualities and utilisations

The energetic qualities of the 16-pointed star are similar to those of the 8-pointed star. The 16-pointed star supports the opening and expansion of the crown chakra and acts as a key to the heavens above. The 8-pointed star activates the birth of Christ Consciousness on an individual level, whereas I use the 16-pointed star for activating and experiencing oneness on a collective level. As I mentioned before (see Chapter 5.11), I experience Christ Consciousness as feeling compassion with all life, seeing the divine light in everyone and everything, thereby experiencing oneness through the True Self – and this is supported by the 16-pointed star.

Please refer to Chapter 7.19 to experience the 16-pointed star.

## 5.13
## 17-Pointed Star

Figure 74: 17-pointed star

### Description

The 17-pointed star can be drawn as a standalone star (see Figure 74).

### Energetic qualities and utilisations

The 17-pointed star marks the journey of transition from the 16-pointed star to the 18-pointed star with their respective energetic qualities and utilisations. In other words, the 17-pointed star facilitates your transition from experiencing oneness with life (reflected by the 16-pointed star) to moving out of old collective paradigms (reflected by the 18-pointed star).

Please refer to Chapter 7.19 to experience the 17-pointed star.

# 5.14
# 18-Pointed Star

Figure 75: 18-pointed star

## Description

The 18-pointed star (see Figure 75) can be drawn in one go or by joining two 9-pointed stars.

## Energetic qualities and utilisations

The energetic qualities of the 18-pointed star are similar to the ones of the 9-pointed star but are of a collective nature. The 18-pointed star facilitates ending old collective paradigms that no longer serve you and stepping out of the so-called old collective "matrix", i.e. the old socio-economic and political paradigms and contexts.

Please refer to Chapter 7.19 to experience the 18-pointed star.

## 5.15
## 22-Pointed Star

Figure 76: 22-pointed star

### Description

The 22-pointed star (see Figure 76) is based on the second master number (22), after the number 11. It bridges the energetic qualities of the 10er star series with a focus on the collective level of humanity on Earth through each and every one of us to the energetic qualities of the 20s with a focus on collective human consciousness related to galactic and universal levels through each and every one of us.

### Energetic qualities and utilisations

The 22-pointed star marks new beginnings on a collective level of humanity, which become possible in the light of the expansion of consciousness on individual and collective levels. It acts as a portal through which we step into our multidimensional nature and act as a human collective in the universe. You start to experience the universe as within you.

Please refer to Chapter 7.19 to experience the 22-pointed star.

# 5.16
# 24-Pointed Star

Figure 77: 24-pointed star

## Description

The 24-pointed star (see Figure 77) can be drawn in one go or by joining three 8-pointed stars or two 12-pointed stars.

## Energetic qualities and utilisations

The 24-pointed star carries the energies of Christ Consciousness – compassion, interconnectedness and oneness with all life – to another level: While the 8-pointed star facilitates this experience on an individual level and the 16-pointed star on the level of humanity, the 24-pointed star supports the experience of oneness with all life on a universal level.

Another perspective on the 24-pointed star is as follows: While the 12-pointed star facilitates living your mastery and calling on a planetary level, the 24-pointed star expands this to a universal level.

Please refer to Chapter 7.19 to experience the 24-pointed star.

## 5.17
## 33-Pointed Star

Figure 78: 33-pointed star

### Description

The 33-pointed star (see Figure 78) carries the third master number 33 and is reflected in the 33 vertebrae of the spine of a human being, which acts like the stem of a Tree of Life.

### Energetic qualities and utilisations

The 33-pointed star marks the expansion of the human collective's consciousness into galactic and universal levels. It carries the energies of limitlessness and "everything is possible" that stem from knowing "thy Self" and expressing the love that we are. Be open for surprises when working with the 33-pointed star.

Please refer to Chapter 7.19 to experience the 33-pointed star.

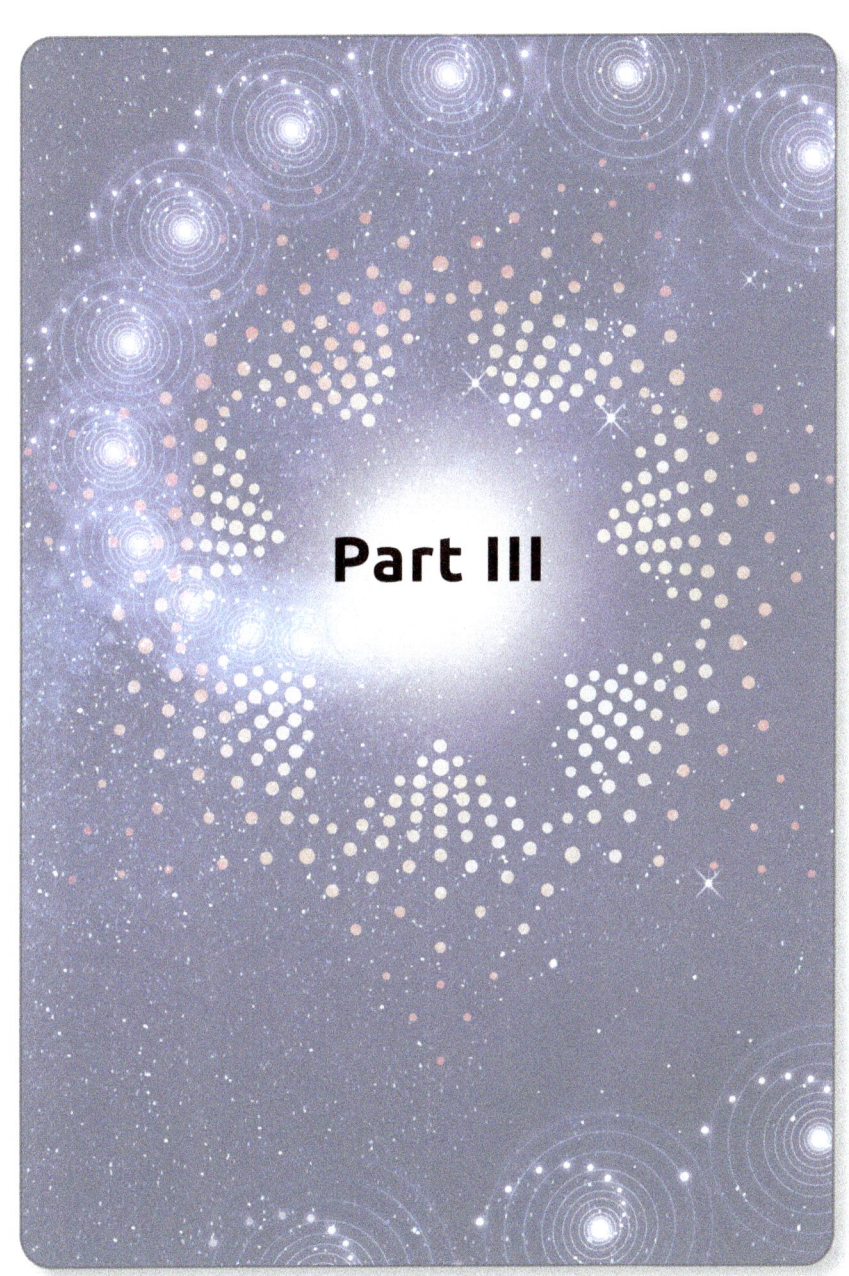

# Part III

Chapter 6

# Ways to Use Sacred Geometry

Figure 79: Create your own sacred geometry design

Below you will find inspirations about how to use sacred geometry physically and/or energetically for everyday life. Familiarise yourself with the options and choose your favourites before diving into the practical tools in Chapter 7.

# 6.1
# Creating and Using Physical Sacred Geometry Objects

- Physical installations of sacred geometry:
  You can build or construct huge three-dimensional sacred geometry forms such as a pyramid or a dodecahedron, using wooden or metal bars, for instance. Another simpler option is to create two-dimensional sacred geometry shapes on the ground, using stones, crystals or threads or simply raking leaves in a geometric pattern. Step into the sacred geometry shape or form and/or invite your friends and clients inside. Connect to your zero-point, ask for the activation of the sacred geometry and meditate or simply stand/sit/lie still while enjoying its energies. You could also use a specific intention with the activation – preferably linked to the energetic qualities of the shape or form (see Chapters 4 and 5).

- Sacred geometry creations:
  Create sacred geometry shapes such as an Ankh, an infinity symbol, a circle or any star with suitable objects such as seeds, fruits, food, crystals or stones. You can step into these shapes as described above or use them for meditative and decorative purposes – or perhaps eat them (see Figure 79)!

- Energising water and food with frequencies of sacred geometry:
  Place your water bottle and/or your food onto your chosen sacred geometry symbol (e.g. Flower of Life, Metatron's Cube) to infuse the water and/or food with these sacred frequencies. You can also stick a sacred geometry symbol on a water bottle or buy water containers with sacred geometry symbols on them. The water – and to a lesser extent the food – will absorb theses frequencies and share them with your cells when they are ingested (see Chapter 3 for a reference on the impact of frequencies on water).

- Sacred geometry on your body:
  Take a physical representation or a printout version of a sacred geometry symbol (preferably as a coloured printout as the colours contain light codes) and put it on specific body parts for a certain time period, or at night, to infuse your cells and the water in your body with the energy and frequencies of that particular image. Thanks to the high content of water in our bodies and the impact of frequencies on water (see reference in Chapter 3), this practice will lead to energetic shifts in your body in accordance with the sacred geometry's energetic properties. You might want to put the printout in foil or use a laminated image for hygienic reasons before placing it on your body. Tattoo lovers might enjoy exploring sacred geometry tattoos!

- Energising your space with sacred geometry codes:
  Place sacred geometry objects and/or images (such as small pyramids and stars) in various places in your house and garden. You can also hang them from ceilings or put them on a spinner to create movement. Perhaps you'd like to energise your flowers and plants with sacred geometry codes by installing geometric forms in your garden and/or by placing a vase with flowers on a sacred geometry shape?

- Sacred geometry in plant and tree formations:
  Plant your garden according to sacred geometry patterns, for instance plant flowerbeds in the form of a pentagram or a 6-pointed or 8-pointed star. You might also choose to plant hedges in the form of a star or plant certain flowers in your favourite sacred geometry patterns to good effect (see Figures 52, 54 and 63).

- Sacred geometry in labyrinths and mazes:
  In gardens used for meditation and near religious and spiritual places there are sometimes labyrinths and mazes built with the use of plants, hedges, rocks and stones. They may be built

according to sacred geometry patterns and designs, such as spiral formations.

- Sacred geometry in architecture:
  There are many ways to use sacred geometry in architecture, including constructing buildings or parts of buildings according to principles of sacred geometry (e.g. using the golden ratio or pi) and/or using sacred geometry forms in the construction (e.g. pentagonal or octagonal rooms). In the interior design, you can use tiles, wallpaper, photos, paintings and/or furniture featuring sacred geometry patterns. Some ancient cities were planned and constructed on the basis of sacred geometry where, for instance, the most important buildings of the city were allocated in the form of a pentagram/pentagon.

- Sacred geometry in art and jewellery:
  You can draw, paint or install sacred geometry shapes and patterns in works of art and either create or buy jewellery (such as pendants, bracelets, rings and earrings) with incorporated sacred geometry symbols.

- Sacred geometry in designs:
  Sacred geometry shapes, forms and patterns can be used in clothing, towels, table sets, china, accessories and jewellery.

- Sacred geometry in games:
  Sacred geometry shapes and forms can be incorporated into both board and computer games.

- Sacred geometry in sounds and music:
  Like sacred geometry, music is also based on mathematics, each sound producing a certain geometric pattern (see, for example, the so-called Chladni figures[23] or a video demonstration by Gregg

---

[23] https://en.wikipedia.org/wiki/Ernst_Chladni#Chladni_figures

Braden[24]). The term "pentagram" in music refers to a stack of five lines and four spaces in which musical notes are recorded. There are many links between music/sounds and geometry. You can also create your own links by, for instance, incorporating the Fibonacci sequence (see Chapter 2) into music through the duration of sounds (e.g. 0; 1; 1; 2; 3; 5; 8; 13; 21; 34; … seconds long) or a sequence of musical notes (e.g. silence; c; c; d; e; g; c; ….) in line with the Fibonacci numbers. Musicians might come up with additional ideas on how to integrate visual sacred geometry into sounds and music.

---

[24] https://www.youtube.com/watch?v=4p7PFHL5W54

## 6.2
# Using Sacred Geometry Energetically

There are many examples and practices of how to use sacred geometry energetically for specific purposes in Chapter 7. Outlined below are general ways of energetic utilisation. You can do them for yourself or – with the other person's consent – for another person, such as a client. If you cannot ask the person directly for his or her consent, ask his or her soul for permission.

- Invite certain sacred geometry shapes and forms into your body and energetic system with the intention of benefitting from the energetic qualities and frequencies of the shape or form. The practices in Chapter 7 recommend the use of specific shapes and forms for many different purposes and intentions. Set a corresponding intention by thinking or saying what you want and ask the sacred geometry shape or form to activate itself and to support you with this. You might want to ask for the rotation of the shape or form and/or for a specific colour. Alternatively, you might prefer to simply observe which rotation or colour – if any – present themselves in the process of the practice.

- Imagine a sacred geometry shape or form in front of you, one large enough for you to step into, and then set the intention to step into its centre. Ask it to activate itself and rotate within, around and through you with a certain intention, which is preferably linked to the energetic qualities and utilisations of that shape or form (see Chapters 4, 5 and 7).

- Install rotating vortices of sacred geometry shapes or forms for certain purposes in your body and energy system. Set a corresponding intention by thinking or saying what you want and ask the sacred geometry vortex to activate itself and support you with this. Visualising the rotating movement of the sacred geometry in action intensifies the process.

Working with vortices generally has stronger, and sometimes more immediate, effects than working with the shape or form alone.

- Install grids of sacred geometry shapes or forms for certain purposes in your body and energy system. Set a corresponding intention by thinking or saying what you want and ask the sacred geometry grid to activate itself and support you with this.

  Working with sacred geometry grids facilitates connections and flow between points in the body and energy system, potentially providing longer energetic effects than working with the shape or form alone.

- Invite a certain sacred geometry into a situation by intention. You might also want to invite the souls of the people involved to connect with that sacred geometry and its qualities and frequencies. For instance, a dodecahedron is particularly useful to bring in grace and universal love to a situation of conflict.

- You can do visionary work with the pentagram or pentagon, for example in the context of constellations, and there is a corresponding practice in Chapter 7.10.

- Choose a specific topic you want support with, state your intention and energetically invite the five Platonic solids one after the other into your body and energetic system to provide this support.

- Combine your coaching and training methods with the energetic properties of sacred geometry.

- Download sacred geometry codes into crystals through your intention for the highest and best good of all concerned.

- Infuse your website and/or your publications with sacred geometry codes through your intention for the highest and best good of all concerned.

- Infuse music with sacred geometry codes through your intention for the highest and best good of all concerned.

- Infuse certain products with sacred geometry codes through your intention for the highest and best good of all concerned.

- By intention, energetically offer sacred geometry symbols to a room or place and ask them to activate themselves, rotate and share their frequencies for the highest and best good of all concerned.

- In the highest and best good of all concerned, offer sacred geometry shapes and forms to the Earth's grid, countries or regions and/or the collective human consciousness through your intention. Simply offer sacred geometry frequencies, never imposing them.

# 6.3
# Meditating with Sacred Geometry

There are many ways to meditate with sacred geometry. Below you will find some inspirations. Many of the practices in Chapter 7 may also be used for meditations. Free meditations and activations are available on my website and social media channels listed in the section "About the author". You will also find links to other resources in Chapter 10.

- Hold a sacred geometry object in your hands or place it in front of you, ask it to activate itself and to show you insights related to a specific topic. I frequently use Metatron's Cube for inspiration and guidance as it supports us in the unfolding of our soul paths. The sphere is a helpful form for visions. Other suitable shapes and forms for insights are the Flower of Life, the dodecahedron, the icosahedron and the 7-pointed and 8-pointed stars.

- Use sacred geometry symbols as background and screen savers on your computer and phone.

- Look at, and meditate with, sacred geometry designs and animations. You will find some on my Instagram page and more in the resources listed in Chapter 10.

- Play with sacred geometry cards for energetic activations as well as for inspiration and guidance. I enjoy using Janosh's sacred geometry cards.[25]

- Look at, and meditate with, crop circles that contain sacred geometry patterns and let yourself be activated by them.

- Go on a journey to other dimensions and realities in your Merkaba (see Chapter 7.14).

---

[25]  www.janosh.com/en

## 6.4
## Embodying Sacred Geometry

- Body as a pentagram:
  Use your body to form a pentagram and experience your essence (see practice in Chapter 7.6).

- Body geometry:
  Use sacred geometry patterns for body movements and observe how they affect your energy system.

  Example from my own experience: I first danced the four Sevillanas (a type of flamenco dance) as usual. Then I set the intention to dance the four Sevillanas in the form of a tetrahedron where my first Sevillana dance represented the first point of a tetrahedron and the second/third/fourth Sevillana dance represented the second/third/fourth point of a tetrahedron, respectively. When I introduced the tetrahedron by intention to the dance, I could feel energy shifts in my body throughout the dance of the four Sevillanas, which I had not perceived before. In alignment with the tetrahedron's energetic properties, I experienced the release of some physical blockages during the tetrahedral dance pattern.

- Human mandala:
  Form a sacred geometry symbol with a group of people and activate it.

  Example from my own experience: With a group of friends we built an 8-pointed star: Four people formed one square facing outwards, while four others formed the second square facing inwards. Some friends went into the star's centre to experience the energies. We connected to our zero-points and felt the power of the energies of our human 8-pointed star and its corresponding energy field and vibrations. When we toned "OM", we felt the energies even more strongly.

# Chapter 7

# Practical Tools for Everyday Topics

Figure 80: Rubik's Cube

## 7.0
## Introduction – Please Read

It's time to activate your highest potential with sacred geometry, are you ready?

Congratulations! You have reached the core of this book. Chapter 7 will provide you with many valuable tools on how to use sacred geometry in everyday life for any topics you might have. I'll present various ways of working with sacred geometry shapes and forms (e.g. inviting a shape/form in, vortex, grid, printout, using multiple shapes and forms) while suggesting different options for your intentions.

Please read Chapter 6 – especially Chapter 6.2 – before starting any of the subsequent practices to familiarise yourself with different ways of using sacred geometry energetically. Please feel free to apply the modalities and intentions you like most to any other practice and shape/form as well. I also invite you to create and add your own modalities and intentions.

To do the practices from a soul connection rather than from the mind, go into your zero-point at the start of each practice. Please refer to Chapter 4.0 for details. Here is a summary of the ways to connect to your zero-point:

- Take a few deep breaths and imagine going down a golden spiral staircase all the way from your mind into the centre of your heart chakra.
- Focus on your zero-point in the middle of your heart chakra.
- Say or think: "I set the intention to connect to my zero-point."
- And breathe into your zero-point.

If it feels more comfortable when inviting sacred geometry shapes and forms into your body and energy system, add "for my highest and best good" or "for the highest and best good of all concerned" when stating your intention. Operating from the zero-point with integrity and a pure intention ensures the highest and best good of all concerned.

Please be aware that you might react to some of the practices and/or the energetics of certain shapes and forms with heat, cold, body sensations, emotions, mental noise and/or headaches. Usually, these symptoms only temporarily accompany the energetic releases and shifts and quickly subside. If they persist, you might want to consult a physician or qualified health care professional to rule out any health challenges.

Repeat the practices over a certain period of time, or for as long as you are guided to do so. Recording your favourite practices on a recording device, so you can follow them with your eyes closed while listening to the instructions, is also helpful.

# 7.1
# From Escaping Your Present Reality
# to Grounding, Earthing and Embodiment

**Hexahedron/Cube:**

The hexahedron (or cube) is a suitable geometric form to help you come fully into your physical body and connect with Earth. It also supports your root chakra. It's helpful to play with when you find it hard to stay present and grounded.

During my personal work with the hexahedron, I felt energy shifts in my root chakra, sinuses and digestion. I felt guided to go hiking in nature, which strengthened my legs and body as well as my connection to Earth. In general, the hexahedron assisted me in feeling more connected to – and present in – my physical body, relaxed and earthed.

Practices:

GROUNDING AND EARTHING:

- Go into your zero-point. Connect with your root chakra at the base of your spine with the help of your breath and tune into your physical body. Ask yourself:

  * Do I feel present in my body?
  * What could assist me in feeling more grounded and connected to Earth?

  Then invite an appropriate type of cube into your body and energy system and ask it to activate itself and support you in grounding and earthing yourself.

  * How does the cube look?
  * What colour is it?
  * Where in your system does it go?

\*   Does it make any movement?

Breathe and relax into its energies.

- Go into your zero-point. Set the intention to form and activate multiple (for instance: 13) hexahedrons one inside the other (like the Russian dolls principle) to support you in coming fully into your physical body and connecting to Earth. Imagine yourself stepping into the innermost centre of all hexahedrons and relax into the energies. Breathe into all your cells and your feet and feel your connection to Earth.

EMBODIMENT:

- Go into your zero-point. Imagine a huge crystalline cube in front of you, reflecting the sunlight. By intention step into it energetically and sit down. Breathe. Ask the cube to activate itself. Feel or sense the presence and protection of the cube around you. Enjoy the silence and the reflection of the sunlight in the cube's crystalline structure and within you. How present do you feel in your body right now?

- Go into your zero-point. Ask for the installation and activation of a hexahedron grid in your energy system and cells with the intention of supporting your Higher Self in coming fully into your body. Breathe and invite yourself in.

You can dive deeper into feeling safe and grounding your purpose through the practices with Metatron's Cube in Chapter 7.8. You might also wish to refer to the practice with the Upside-Down Ankh (Chapter 7.15 a) for a deeper connection to Earth.

## 7.2
## From Emotional Turbulence
## to Emotional Balance

**Icosahedron:**

The icosahedron is a suitable geometric form to transmute emotional pain and balance the emotions, while supporting the flow of energy, the letting go of the old and making space for the new. It assists with trust, insights and uplifting connections to other people.

I recommend connecting to the icosahedron on a daily basis in emotionally turbulent times and whenever you feel emotionally challenged or stuck.

Practices:

EMOTIONAL BALANCE:

• Go into your zero-point in the middle of your heart chakra and breathe. Imagine you can see, sense or feel an icosahedron right in front of you – one large enough for you to step into. Set the intention to step into the centre of this icosahedron. You might want to connect to your sacral chakra just below your navel and to your emotions. Ask the icosahedron to activate itself and rotate within and around you. Ask it to support you in balancing your emotions and flowing with life. Relax and breathe deeply. Experience the energies. Do you feel more emotionally balanced now?

• Go into your zero-point. By using your intention, install an icosahedron vortex in your energy system, especially with respect to your emotions. For example, you might state your intention as follows: "I call for the installation and activation of an icosahedron vortex in my energy body to balance my emotions and to transmute emotional pain into love." Feel the energies.

Visualise how the vortex swirls around in your energy system, transmuting old emotions and bringing about balance in your energy body.

When working with the icosahedron in this way, I experienced sadness, anger and frustration, sometimes triggered by daily events. I also felt the clearing of energetic blockages and the renewed flow of energies. Synchronicities often occurred later that day or week.

RENEWAL:

Go into your zero-point. You might want to look at or hold an icosahedron in your hands. Ask your guides and angels to install and activate an icosahedron grid with rotating icosahedrons in your energy system, directed at purifying and renewing your challenging emotional experiences. Breathe deeply and let the icosahedrons do their work.

During this practice, I saw a beautiful diamond white light appear in my energy system. The energy shifted, leaving me feeling renewed and upgraded.

ENERGY FLOW:

Go into your zero-point. Place a physical icosahedron or a printout of an icosahedron on your abdomen, your lower back, on the area between the heart chakra and the throat chakra or wherever guided during your sleep, or for some time during the day, to improve the energy flow in your body.

FLOW IN YOUR LIFE:

Go into your zero-point. Invite an icosahedron vortex into your energetic system, ask it to activate itself and to move and rotate within and around you. Ask yourself the following questions:

* How do I feel?
* Are my emotions balanced?
* Is my life in flow?
* What do I want to let go of?
* What am I passionate about?
* Which emotions or creative endeavours of mine want to flow?

Ask the icosahedron vortex to support you with this flow in your life. Breathe deeply and experience its energies.

FINETUNING YOUR CONTACTS:

Go into your zero-point. Meditate with an icosahedron while feeling or imagining that you ARE the icosahedron. Notice your many contact points with the outer world. The icosahedron is made of 20 triangles, 12 corners and 30 edges. Then ask yourself the following questions:

* Where is my place? Where is my area?
* Where is the area of others?

This helps you to define your space and to set boundaries.

Ask for insights about the following topics:

* Which of my relationships flow like water?
* Where do I encounter barriers and frontiers?
* What can I do to attract and form relationships that nurture both me and the others involved?

Ask the icosahedron to support you with whatever changes you desire in relation to your contacts.

# 7.3
# From Physical Challenges to
# Improved Health and Well-Being

Figure 81: Tetrahedron

**Tetrahedron:**

The tetrahedron is a suitable geometric form to assist in restoring physical balance and improving health and well-being. Due to its fiery energy and focused approach it helps to free stuck energies, preparing the way for a new energy flow.

Using the tetrahedron (vortex) in a number of cases, I find it particularly useful for boosting the immune system, metabolism and digestion (for example, in the case of constipation), activating sexual energy and working with teeth. Yet, in order to address inflammation in the body, I would rather use the icosahedron with its watery energy, or the multi-faceted Cosmic Egg, than the fiery tetrahedron. In order to experience lasting improvements, repeat these practices over a certain time period.

Practices:

PHYSICAL BALANCE:

• Go into your zero-point. You might want to tune into your body first, screen it and ask yourself: "Which parts of my physical body and energetic system need balance and support now?" For instance, you could work with your immune system, digestion, teeth, sexuality, with the critical inner voice in your head or with almost any part of your body that feels out of balance. By using your intention, energetically install a tetrahedron vortex or a tetrahedron grid in the parts of your body or energetic system you want support with. Breathe, relax and visualise or sense how the energies do their work.

Here are some examples:
* IMMUNE SYSTEM: Say your intention, feel the energies and/or visualise the tetrahedron grid: "I call for the installation and activation of a tetrahedron grid in my energy system directed at boosting my immune system."
* STIMULATING YOUR DIGESTION (when suffering from constipation): Say your intention, feel the energies and/or visualise the tetrahedron vortex in action: "I call for the installation and activation of a tetrahedron vortex in my bowel with the intention of bringing about a healthy and gentle intestinal voiding now."
* SEXUALITY: Say your intention, feel the energies and/or visualise the tetrahedron vortex in action: "I call for the installation and activation of a tetrahedron vortex in my second chakra to activate my sexual energies in a balanced way."
* TEETH: Say your intention, feel the energies and/or visualise the tetrahedron vortices in action: "I call for the installation, activation and rotation of an Earth tetrahedron vortex in each tooth in my lower jaw, and I call for the installation, activation and rotation of a Sun tetrahedron vortex in each tooth in my upper jaw with the intention of restoring balance and harmony in my teeth and related areas".[26]

---

[26] For an explanation of Earth and Sun tetrahedrons please refer to Chapter 4.6.3.

- Place a physical tetrahedron or a printout of a tetrahedron on a specific body part either during sleep or for some time during the day.

I noticed strong energetic shifts when placing a printout of a golden tetrahedron on my spine between my tailbone and sacrum. When placing it on my digestive tract, it helped to speed up my metabolic system and digestion.

**Other useful sacred geometry forms for health and well-being – Hexahedron, Icosahedron, Cosmic Egg:**

The following forms can also support health and well-being in specific areas; repeat the practices as guided:

- Hexahedron (earth element): Digestion, purification and de-acidification of the physical body
- Icosahedron (water element): Circulation of blood and other bodily fluids, soothing inflammation in the body
- Cosmic Egg: Return to harmony and well-being on many levels of the physical and energetic body

Practices:

SUPPORTING YOUR DIGESTION WITH THE HEXAHEDRON:

- Place a physical hexahedron or a printout of a hexahedron onto your stomach, liver and digestive system either during sleep or for some time during the day. Breathe deeply.

- Go into your zero-point. Set the intention to install and activate a crystalline hexahedron vortex in your stomach, liver and digestive system, asking it to detox, purify and de-acidify your physical body and cells. Visualise the rotation of the hexahedron vortex and its effects in those areas. Repeat this practice as guided.

In my personal work with the hexahedron over several weeks, my digestion improved. You might want to play with it while undergoing a detox and purification of your physical body.

## SUPPORTING BLOOD CIRCULATION WITH THE ICOSA-HEDRON:

Go into your zero-point. By using your intention, energetically install and activate an icosahedron grid in certain parts of your body or energetic system. Say your intention, feel the energies and/or visualise the icosahedron grid. Using the example of joint pain: "I call for the installation and activation of an icosahedron grid in my joints with the intention of improving the blood circulation, movement and flexibility in my joints."

## SUPPORTING THE FUNCTIONING OF THE LYMPHATIC SYSTEM WITH THE ICOSAHEDRON:

Go into your zero-point. Say your intention, feel the energies and/ or visualise the icosahedron grid: "I call for the installation and activation of an icosahedron grid in my lymphatic system with the intention of supporting its functioning, e.g. regarding the removal of cellular waste from my body."

## RESTORING HARMONY AND WELL-BEING ON MANY LEVELS WITH THE COSMIC EGG:

Go into your zero-point. By intention ask for the installation of a Cosmic Egg grid system in your body and cells on cellular, molecular, particle, atomic and quantum levels. Request the activation and rotation of the Cosmic Eggs with the intention of clearing and transforming all the energies, information and cellular imprints that no longer serve you, as well as of restoring harmony and well-being on all levels of your body and cells. Relax into the energies and breathe. Imagine a purifying white light entering all your cells. See, sense or feel the energetic and physical shifts that support the process.

## 7.4
## From Exhaustion to Higher Energy Levels

**Tetrahedron:**

The tetrahedron is excellent for boosting the immune and digestive systems (see Chapter 7.3), increasing energy and activity levels and improving well-being, particularly when feeling exhausted, lethargic and depleted. The tetrahedron brings fiery energy to the body and energy system.

Practices:

RAISING ENERGY LEVELS:

Go into your zero-point. State your intention and feel the energies: "I call for the installation and activation of a tetrahedron grid in my energy system to raise my energies and to activate my energy body for as long as it is for my highest and best good." Repeat this practice for as long as guided and notice any difference in your energy levels.

I worked with the tetrahedron in this way every morning and evening for three weeks and felt fiery and more active during that time. I managed to finish a project and then moved on to explore the next geometry.

COMING INTO ACTION:

Go into your zero-point. Connect to your solar plexus chakra located in the upper abdomen and feel your energy body. Invite a tetrahedron vortex into your energetic system and ask it to activate itself and to rotate within and around you. Ask yourself the following questions:

* What drives me every day in life?
* How can I step into my power and achieve my goals?

Ask the tetrahedron vortex to support you in raising your passion, energy and action levels.

**Pyramid:**

The pyramid energy helps to increase energy levels and the vibration of the energetic system. It also supports you in protecting yourself against outside influences.

Practices:

RAISING YOUR ENERGY LEVELS:

Go into your zero-point and breathe. Invite a pyramid into your body and energy system, asking it to activate itself and to rotate and spin within, around and through you with the intention of raising your energy levels. Breathe. What do you notice?

UPLIFTING YOUR ENERGIES:

Go into your zero-point and breathe, closing your eyes if this feels comfortable. See, sense or feel a golden pyramid in front of you. Imagine stepping into the pyramid's centre through a gate that is opening up in front of you. Relax into the pyramid's golden frequency. Invite the pyramid's golden energy to flow into every cell of your body with the intention of increasing your energy levels and the vibration of your energetic system. Do you feel uplifted?

You might want to do this practice during a mid-afternoon slump or when feeling exhausted. It's a good alternative to reaching for caffeine or sugar to pick you up. I always feel uplifted when working with a golden pyramid.

## PROTECTION AGAINST OUTSIDE INFLUENCES:

Go into your zero-point and breathe. You might want to close your eyes. See, sense or feel a golden pyramid in front of you. Imagine that you step into the pyramid's centre through a gate that is opening up in front of you. Relax into the pyramid's golden frequency. Invite the pyramid's golden energy to flow within, through and around you with the intention of protecting you from any outside influences. Do you feel sheltered?

You might want to invite a second golden pyramid – which is a mirror image of the first one – to come up from Inner Earth to connect with the first pyramid, forming an octahedron. Imagine yourself in the centre where both pyramids intersect. Invite the golden energies of both pyramids to flow within, around and through you with the intention of protecting you from any outside influences. Do you now feel sheltered and grounded at the same time?

You can do this practice when you go to busy places, especially if you are sensitive to energies around you.

I invite you to also check out a practice with the Kundalini Ankh to activate your life force and kundalini energy in Chapter 7.15 c).

# 7.5
# From Confusion to Mental Clarity and Focus

**Octahedron:**

The octahedron is a suitable geometric form to clear mental confusion and imbalances and to activate clarity and focus within, bringing its airy energy to your body and energy system.

During my personal work with the octahedron, my (mental) plans changed. I was invited to be with what was unfolding and to live in the moment. I also experienced an upgrade of my nervous system, which was accompanied by a headache for a day.

Practices:

MAKING SPACE IN YOUR PHYSICAL BODY:

Place a physical octahedron or a printout of an octahedron on your head, lungs, heart chakra or spine during sleep or for some time during the day.

CLARITY AND FOCUS:

Go into your zero-point. State: "I call for the installation and activation of an octahedron vortex in my mind and energy system with the intention of dissolving any mental confusion, as well as old programmes and patterns that no longer serve me. I ask the octahedron vortex to help me strengthen my clarity and focus." Visualise the swirling octahedron, then tune into the energy. Where in your body do you feel any shifts? What has changed? What is ready to be revealed?

I felt the octahedron as a whirlwind in my energy system, especially in my head. It left me clearer and lighter afterwards – with more space within me.

OPENING YOU UP FOR YOUR HEART'S WISDOM AND JOY:

Go into your zero-point and connect to your heart chakra. Imagine you can see, sense or feel a large octahedron in front of you. Set the intention to step into its centre. Ask the octahedron to activate itself and rotate within, around and through you with the intention of clearing your mind and mental patterns for your highest good. Ask it to support you on your journey from your head to your heart while activating ease, joy and playfulness. Breathe and relax into the energies. What do you experience?

CLEARING SPACES:

Use physical or energetic octahedrons to clear spaces by walking around the spaces stating the following intention from your zero-point: "I call for the installation and activation of an octahedron grid in this place to clear all the old energies and bring in fresh air, more space and light."

You can further enhance your clarity and focus through the practices with Metatron's Cube in Chapter 7.8.

# 7.6
# From Judgment of Yourself and Others to Compassion and Grace

Figure 82: Dodecahedron

**Pentagram – for a personal perspective:**

The pentagram opens your heart to love and compassion towards yourself and takes you home to your essence. In this way, it also supports you in releasing self-criticism and self-judgment.

**10-pointed star – from a personal to a joint perspective:**

The 10-pointed star helps you experience your essence with and through the essence of another person and facilitates the co-creation of something new.

**Dodecahedron – for a collective perspective:**

The dodecahedron opens the heart, facilitates connection to higher realms and telepathic communication with all forms of life and is supportive in expanding consciousness and experiencing universal love and grace.

It's beneficial to first work with the pentagram before moving on to the 10-pointed star and the dodecahedron.

Practices:

**Pentagram:**

RELEASING DENSITY:

Place a physical pentagram or a printout of a pentagram on a specific body part during sleep or for some time during the day.

When I worked with the pentagram in this way, I felt pressure and subsequent energy shifts in areas of my body which still held density and stuck energies, such as the throat, neck and liver. I also experienced an opening of my heart chakra.

ACTIVATING AND EXPANDING YOUR ESSENCE (SOUL):

I invite you to stand up and form a pentagram with your body: Hold your head straight and look forward with your arms outstretched in a horizontal line at shoulder height; position your legs a little more than hip-width apart (see Leonardo Da Vinci's Vitruvian (hu-)man in Chapter 5.1). Go into your zero-point and breathe. Close your eyes if you wish to. Set the intention to activate the pentagram within you. See, sense or feel how the energy of your essence (soul) flows from your heart centre into all five points of the star located in your head, hands and feet. Expand your essence through your intention, focus and breath until you see, sense or feel it everywhere in your body. If you feel energetic blocks in certain body parts, allow your body wisdom to make the appropriate movements to unblock the energy flow. Breathe into your essence. When you feel fully nourished with your essence, radiate the love that you are from your zero-point out into the world.

This could be a great practice to do with children as a way of encouraging them to feel and share their essence. The 5-pointed star is often featured on children's clothes, backpacks and accessories these days which might amplify this experience for them.

ECSTACY FOR LIFE:

Go into your zero-point. By intention, install a pentagram vortex inside, asking it to open you up to the ecstasy for life. Then imagine yourself as a 5-pointed star (see picture of the Vitruvian (hu-)man in Chapter 5.1 and the practice above) guided by the heart, spinning faster and faster while anchoring ecstasy through the two feet of your "star". Your body might want to move during this practice.

**10-pointed star:**

EXPERIENCING YOUR ESSENCE IN THE WORLD:

Go into your zero-point. Activate your essence (see second pentagram practice above) and set the intention to energetically communicate with the essence of another person of your choice. Imagine the other person's essence reflected in another pentagram outside of you. Engage in a dance of the two pentagrams for a while until both your energy bodies – with a little rotation – merge into a 10-pointed star. Ask the 10-pointed star to rotate within and around your energy system with the intention of activating unity consciousness within you. Relax into the energies.

**Dodecahedron:**

EXPERIENCING GRACE AND UNIVERSAL LOVE:

Go into your zero-point in the middle of your heart chakra and breathe. You might want to close your eyes. Imagine you can see, sense or feel a dodecahedron right in front of you – one large enough for you to step into. You can also ask your guides and angels to form one or multiple dodecahedron(s) for you, one inside the other (according to the Russian dolls principle). Set the intention to step into the centre of the (innermost) dodecahedron. Ask the dodecahedron(s) to activate itself/themselves and rotate within and around you, sharing its/their energies of grace and universal love with you. Breathe in deeply and bask in the energies you are sensing. Do you feel peace and an expansion in your heart chakra?

I recommend connecting to the dodecahedron in this way when you wake up – so you can start your day off in harmony with yourself – as well as at the end of the day as an act of appreciation and gratitude to yourself and your day. This practice is also a very helpful tool when you feel down or lonely. You might want to try it out with 33 dodecahedrons.

EXPRESSING LOVE:

Go into your zero-point. Invite a dodecahedron vortex into your energetic system to bring in universal love and grace. Ask it to activate itself and start moving. See, sense or feel how the dodecahedron vortex rotates within you and shares its gifts. Then tune in: How can you express your love today and share it with others?

In working with the dodecahedron, my clients felt peace, love, warmth and stillness, as well as an expansion of the heart chakra and a clearing of the throat chakra. The dodecahedron is my favourite Platonic solid as it facilitates our connection with ALL THAT IS. It reminds us of who we truly are: DIVINE.

TELEPATHIC COMMUNICATION:

Go into your zero-point. Imagine yourself inside a dodecahedron and another person or being inside a second one, letting the two dodecahedrons touch. Connect to the other person or being through the zero-point in the middle of your heart chakra. Start communicating telepathically with the other by focusing on your pineal gland near the centre of your brain behind your third eye. Be open to what emerges in the conversation or afterwards.

UPGRADING YOUR AURA:

Go into your zero-point. Ask for the installation and activation of a dodecahedron grid in your aura to repair and fill up the holes and subtle etheric layers that need tending with universal love and grace. Can you feel the universal love and grace coming in? Now ask for the universal love and grace to be anchored into your auric field.

You might also wish to do the practice with the Illuminated Ankh, which spreads grace and universal love, in Chapter 7.15 e).

# 7.7
# From Repeating Old Patterns to New Beginnings

**Octahedron:**

The spinning octahedron brings fresh air to your mind and opens you to your heart's wisdom and joy.

Practice:

RELEASING THE OLD AND BRINGING IN THE NEW:

Go into your zero-point. Imagine yourself inside a rotating crystalline octahedron connecting heaven and Earth. Ask the octahedron to support you in releasing any old energies and programmes that do not serve you anymore, possibly relating to a specific area in your life. Exhale the old energies into the Earth below. Ask the rotating octahedron to help you bring ease, joy and playfulness into your energy system while breathing in fresh energy from above (heaven) into all your cells and chakras. Now breathe out the old energies, again into the Earth below. Continue the process until you feel clearer, lighter and more joyful.

**Merkaba:**

The Merkaba supports you in completing and clearing old patterns and connections to the outside world as well as in bringing new information and codes into your light body.

Practices:

CLEARING YOUR MERKABA:

Go into your zero-point and breathe. Build your personal Merkaba in front of you as a physical 6-pointed star or energetically through intention. Step into the centre of your personal Merkaba, or set the intention to build your personal Merkaba field around you. Feel its energy and vibration. Focus on the living intelligent light field in and around you. See, sense or feel the Earth tetrahedron that grounds you and also the Sun tetrahedron that connects you to the universe. Now see, sense or feel how both poles come together as one in your torso and how you become aligned with the Earth and the Sun at the same time. Breathe deeply with the intention of expanding and experiencing your light body. Your Merkaba is now activated.

Ask your soul for the deletion of old programmes which no longer serve you. Visualise, sense or feel crystalline white light flowing into your Merkaba from above, flowing around you and going down through your energy field into the Earth, washing away old information and programming.

## CLEARING OLD CONNECTIONS:

You can also engage in a more thorough clearing of your Merkaba which, in turn, clears your light body and your personal energy field.

Go into your zero-point. You might want to do the above-mentioned clearing practice first. See, sense or feel your personal Merkaba field around you. Tune into it. In particular, check the eight points of the Merkaba, which reach out to the outside world. They represent your connections to other people, beings, fields, systems and grids. Tune in:

* Which areas of your Merkaba need clearing?
* Where is the energy not flowing?
* How do you perceive your contact points with others?
* Are there ties that bind?

From your zero-point in the middle of your heart chakra, let crystalline white light flow through your Merkaba field and into its points with the intention of clearing any energies and connections that no longer serve you. The Merkaba might rotate during this process. You can also ask for support from the Earth's crystalline energies. Take your time for this clearing. Keep breathing. Stay relaxed so the energies can do their work.

REPROGRAMMING YOUR MERKABA:

Go into your zero-point. Please clear your Merkaba first with one or both practices listed above. Once your Merkaba is cleared, ask your soul to programme your Merkaba with "I Love You". Say it out loud to yourself several times and bask in the energies of love. It is YOU who loves YOU. Authentic self-love is so important and – in my opinion – a prerequisite to truly loving another person, your life and the world. You can also set the intention to programme your Merkaba with your heart's desires.

**Cosmic Egg:**

The powerful Cosmic Egg with all its elements supports you in letting go of the old and stepping into the new.

Practice:

LETTING GO OF THE OLD AND STEPPING INTO THE NEW:

Go into your zero-point. Invite the golden Cosmic Egg into your energy system, asking it to activate itself and rotate in your energy system with the intention of letting go on all levels of old energies and patterns that no longer serve you. See, sense or feel the energy shifts within you. After a while, ask the Cosmic Egg to support you in stepping into the new. Tune in: What is now ready to emerge?

**9-pointed star:**

The 9-pointed star supports you in completing and releasing old patterns in a powerful way. Take your time to go through this process and be gentle with yourself as the practices might bring up issues.

In my group work with the 9-pointed star, we decided to add the words "with ease and grace" to the request of completion because the effects of the 9-pointed star's rotation were very strong for some people.

Practices:

## COMPLETING OLD PATTERNS:

Go into your zero-point. Choose a pattern that is no longer serving you and which you are ready to release. Here are some examples of belief patterns: "I'm not good enough." "I have to work hard to advance in life." "I don't matter in this world." Alternatively, ask your soul to activate such a pattern within you. Ask this pattern to show itself in your body and energy system and see, sense or feel it. Once you perceive this pattern within you, set the intention to step into a 9-pointed star in front of you, which is formed of three interlocking equilateral triangles. Ask the three triangles of the 9-pointed star to rotate and move in different directions in order to clear and complete that pattern within you with ease and grace, in a way that you can handle well. Experience the rotations of the three triangles and the pulsation of their energies. Breathe. During the process, I invite you to follow the leadership of your body: Sounds might want to come out. Your body might want to release toxins through yawning, or it may want to move. Keep going until the 9-pointed star comes to a complete standstill and feel and know that the pattern in your energetic system has been cleared and completed.

## SMASHING WALLS OF PROTECTION:

Go into your zero-point. Imagine a multidimensional 9-pointed star in front of you, one big enough for you to step into. Set the intention to step into the centre of the 9-pointed star and feel its energy. Connect to a situation or a topic, which has led you to build walls of protection around yourself. Visualise, sense or feel those walls of protection. Invite the energy and frequencies of the 9-pointed star into these walls with the intention of smashing them, asking it to rotate anti-clockwise around and into them. See, sense or feel the walls tumbling down and being flattened. Breathe and let the process unfold. Then ask your soul to take care of the remnants of the walls. Once they're completely smashed, ask the 9-pointed star to rotate clockwise around your energy field to seal the completion of this work.

Here are some additional tips for this practice:

- You might want to ask your inner child to help you bring down these walls.
- You can also use the wall metaphor to complete and smash certain patterns in your energy system that aren't serving you, such as "I'm not good enough" or "I don't matter".
- You can go back to your original shutdown and the consequent building of walls and demolish them, or you can do the work in stages by repeating the practice various times until all the walls have been completely removed.
- You might visualise a 9-pointed star with 3 triangles which represent anger/rage (triangle 1), depression (triangle 2) and fear (triangle 3) and focus on releasing or transmuting these emotions simultaneously.
- Take your time and add the words "with ease and grace" to your request if the practice brings up too many emotions and issues.

You will find more practices for destroying old energies and limitations with the Burning Ankh in Chapter 7.15 b) as well as for full-circling the old and stepping into the new with the infinity symbol in Chapter 7.16.

# 7.8
# From Insecurity to More Safety, Focus and Purpose with Metatron's Cube

Figure 83: Metatron's Cube

**Metatron's Cube:**

Metatron's Cube offers stability and strength, protection and structure as well as clarity, certainty and focus. It supports you in bringing ideas and visions that are in alignment with your soul plan into a form and structure, allowing for the manifestation of a higher purpose.

Practices:

PHYSICAL CLEARING OF DENSITY:

Place a physical template or printout version of Metatron's Cube on certain body parts. I recommend placing it on your spine with the central circle on the vertebra opposite the navel, or on your belly with the central circle on the navel itself.

I experienced powerful energetic releases along my spine, up to my head and out of my crown chakra as well as clearing in my sinuses and digestive system when placing the centre of Metatron's Cube on the spine opposite my navel. Placing it on my navel led to energy shifts in my belly and intestines.

## PROTECTED SPACE FOR TRANSFORMATION:

Go into your zero-point. By intention energetically set up Metatron's Cube as a protected space for inner transformation. You may either step inside this space yourself or invite a client in. Ask Metatron's Cube to activate its safeguarding energies and hold a space for deep inner transformation around you or your client. Now you can continue your usual practice in that protected space.

I recommend using this framework-setting practice at the beginning of your transformative work on yourself or with a client.

## ANCHORING STABILITY AND FOCUS:

Go into your zero-point. Call Metatron's Cube into your energy field and into your life, ask it to activate itself and to provide stability and focus in challenging and overwhelming situations. See, sense or feel the cubical structure around you and the comforting and protective energies it exudes. Connect with Metatron's Cube on a daily basis to keep these frequencies alive.

## SHIFTING INTO YOUR INNER CORE:

Go into your zero-point. Meditate with Metatron's Cube and connect with its energies. Focus on the heart of Metatron's Cube, the central circle. Set the intention to energetically step into its centre. Ask Metatron's Cube to activate itself and rotate around, within and through you with the intention of activating your soul path and purpose. See, sense or feel a shift in experience from the outer world to your inner core. Breathe deeply. Tune in: What wants to be revealed right now? Remain in these energies for as long as you wish.

## GAINING CLARITY ABOUT YOUR SOUL'S PRIORITIES:

Set up a huge Metatron's Cube in front of you. You can do it physically by drawing the corresponding circles of the Fruit of Life (the basic structure of Metatron's Cube, see Figure 31) and lines on the ground, by using a printout of Metatron's Cube (see Figure 32) to step onto, or creating it with pebbles, seeds or any other adequate elements. You can also create Metatron's Cube energetically by intention and through your mind's eye. Go into your zero-point. Step into the innermost circle of Metatron's Cube, which represents your soul, and ask for Metatron's Cube to be activated. Ask your soul to reveal its priorities or heart's desires to you with the help of Metatron's Cube. From the central circle (= your soul), step into one of the circles of the inner ring and pause. Ask for insights on the first item of your soul's priorities or heart's desires. Wait until you receive an answer in the form of a word or phrase, an image, a feeling or a knowing. From there, step into the adjacent circle of the outer ring and ask for the next step(s) to bring about that particular soul's priority or heart's desire and wait for an answer. When you have completed the first item, go back into the centre of Metatron's Cube. From there, continue the same process of inquiry by stepping into the next circle of the inner ring and, later on, to the outer ring in order to gain clarity about the second item of your soul's priorities or heart's desires. Keep going until you have completed all six circles of the inner ring with the corresponding outer circles. Now you have an overview of the six main priorities of your soul or your six main heart's desires as well as of the next steps to take. At the end, step into the central circle again and ask for the support of Metatron's Cube in anchoring all these insights and frequencies into your energetic system in the present moment.

You might want to write down your findings or use a recording device while you go through this process. Celebrate your newly gained clarity and begin the first steps in putting your soul plan into action.

LIVING YOUR HIGHER PURPOSE:

Go into your zero-point. Meditate with Metatron's Cube and connect with its energies. Ask for insights and clarity about your higher purpose. Invite Metatron's Cube into your energy system and ask it to activate itself and support you in creating a framework for living your purpose, for example by setting up a daily or weekly structure and accomplishing tasks related to your higher purpose.

BEING YOUR HIGHER PURPOSE:

Go into your zero-point. By intention activate Metatron's Cube within you and feel its energies. Breathe deeply. Set the intention to expand your consciousness until you see, sense, feel or know that you are your higher purpose. Connect to the heart of Metatron's Cube within you, to your zero-point in the middle of your heart chakra, and feel the energies of universal love. See, sense or feel how you emanate the codes of universal love out from your centre (zero-point) to the inner ring of circles of Metatron's Cube within you, on to the outer ring of circles of Metratron's Cube within you and beyond to the world at large. Can you feel that you are your higher purpose, that you are LOVE?

# 7.9
# From Surviving to Thriving

**Merkaba:**

The Merkaba is a wonderful geometric form to raise your energy levels in your entire energy system as well as your vibration to take you out of survival consciousness. When you change your vibration, you change your life!

Practice:

ACTIVATING NEW POSSIBILITIES:

You might want to first do (some of) the Merkaba practices of clearing and reprogramming your light body listed in Chapter 7.7 before continuing with this practice.

Go into your zero-point and breathe. Build your personal Merkaba as a physical 6-pointed star in front of you or energetically through intention. Step into the centre of your personal Merkaba, or set the intention to build your personal Merkaba field around you. Feel its energy and vibration. Focus on the living intelligent light field in and around you. See, sense or feel the Earth tetrahedron that grounds you, and the Sun tetrahedron connecting you to the universe. See, sense or feel how both poles come together as one in your torso and how you become aligned with the Earth and the Sun at the same time.

Breathe deeply with the intention of expanding and experiencing your light body. Perceive how your energy levels rise with each breath. Now ask your Merkaba to start rotating at the frequency which serves you best right now in energising you and raising your vibration. Be aware that the Earth and Sun tetrahedrons might rotate in different directions and/or at different speeds. Let the Merkaba spin for some time and breathe into the process. Then tune into your energy system: How do you feel? What becomes possible now?

Write down your insights. Be aware that this process might also swirl issues up to the surface. So, use this practice and the spinning of the Merkaba as guided and ask your soul to help you deal with anything arising.

You might wonder how changing your vibration changes your life. Let me give you an example from my Merkaba experience: I recorded a guided Merkaba meditation practice where I activated my personal Merkaba as presented above, cleared it of old energies and reprogrammed it with self-love (see Chapter 7.7). After listening to the meditation a couple of times, I felt more love for myself and others and was inspired to take up certain activities again which I really enjoy.

**Cosmic Egg:**

The Cosmic Egg combines all the qualities and effects of the five Platonic solids and the Merkaba, working simultaneously on many levels in the order and combinations to best serve you. It supports your expansion, thriving and creative endeavours.

In working with the Cosmic Egg with clients, I noticed that it works wherever in your body and energy system and on whatever topics serve you best in every moment. I experienced energetic shifts in my physical body, emotional releases and dreams about patterns that did not serve me anymore, as well as changes in my thoughts and mental patterns (after asking for clarity and freedom from mental limitations). Clients emerged anew after a phase of depressive tendencies and experienced renewed harmony in certain body parts following accidents.

The general impact of the Cosmic Egg was shown to me in the following image: The Cosmic Egg cleared the layers of fog around a lit candle until a heart formed around the light and the essence of the candle became visible and accessible again.

Practices:

## RETURN TO HARMONY:

Place the Cosmic Egg, or a printout of one, on certain body parts to support you in restoring harmony both to them and/or related areas. You can also ask the Cosmic Egg to suck in all dense energies and transform them into light.

## SUPPORT WITH AN INTENTION OR AS GUIDED:

Meditate with the Cosmic Egg while rotating it in your hands as guided or sitting below or next to a Cosmic Egg spinning from the ceiling or on a spinner. The movement of the Cosmic Egg increases its interaction with your energetic field and produces a stronger energetic effect than when remaining still. Spinning it on different axes will provide you with different energies and access to different portals. Go into your zero-point and set an intention, or allow it to work on its own as guided, supporting you in your current transformation process.

## REMEMBER YOUR TRUE SELF:

Point the Cosmic Egg's centre (where all geometries meet, see Figure 30) to your zero-point, asking the Cosmic Egg to activate itself and rotate within, around and through you with the intention of clearing old and/or stuck energies and transforming them into light. Ask the Cosmic Egg to help you remember your True Self and your original blueprint of creation.

## SUPPORT WITH THRIVING:

Go into your zero-point. Imagine yourself sitting IN a huge golden Cosmic Egg and feel its energies within and around you. Ask the Cosmic Egg to activate itself and to rotate within, around and through you with the intention of facilitating you thriving in life.

**Flower of Life:**

The Flower of Life can awaken your playful and creative inner child.

Practices:

PLAYING IN THE GARDEN OF EDEN:

Go into your zero-point and connect to your inner child. See, sense or feel a huge Flower of Life in front of you. By intention, energetically step into its very centre. Ask the petals of the Flower of Life to activate themselves and to rotate around, within and through you in a playful way. Can you see any colours, hear or feel the airy breeze of the flower's movements or smell a fragrance? How does your inner child experience the flower? Enjoy the magic. Do you feel like a fairy in the Garden of Eden?

CREATING UPON CREATION:

Go into your zero-point. See, sense or feel a huge multidimensional unbounded Flower of Life in front of you. By intention, energetically step into the centre of its innermost sphere and ask the Flower of Life to activate itself. Relax into the perfection of the present moment and the truth of who you are. From there see, sense or feel how the centre of the Flower of Life expands into its first ring of spheres, then into the next ring and so on. Breathe into your own expansion of your energy field. Do you feel your limitless nature and your inherent creativity? Ask yourself the following questions:

* In which areas are harmony and peace restored?
* What becomes possible in my life now?
* What do I want to create?

Use this momentum to take the first action steps.

Please also refer to Chapter 7.15 d) for a practice with the Golden-White Ankh which supports you in your transmutation, purification and the activation of your essence.

SABINE KRUSE

# 7.10
# From Fulfilling Other People's Expectations
# to Following Your Heart's Desires

**Sphere:**

The sphere is a suitable geometric form to facilitate insights and to support you in creating your heart's desires. It also connects you to your inner child, its innocence and playfulness and brings harmony to your relationship with your mother and Mother Earth.

During my personal work with the sphere, I saw various aspects of a vision for my life and felt vibrant and excited about putting it into practice. More and more aspects of my vision have been unfolding ever since.

Practices:

HARMONISING YOUR MOTHER RELATIONSHIP:

Go into your zero-point. Connect with your inner child. See, sense or feel a huge sphere in front of you. Set the intention to energetically step into the sphere's centre. Ask the sphere to activate itself and rotate, spin and move with the intention of supporting your inner child and yourself in harmonising any unresolved topics you might have with your mother and/or Mother Earth. See, sense or feel how the sphere's frequencies spin around and through you until harmony is restored in your energy system. Breathe. Is there any message from your inner child for you, possibly in relation to your mother and/or Mother Earth?

INSIGHTS:

Find a suitable (crystalline) sphere, hold it in your hands, perhaps rolling it around from time to time, and connect with it energetically. Instead of holding a physical sphere, you can also invite an etheric sphere into your energy field or see it in your mind's eye by intention. Go into your zero-point. Connect with the stillness in your zero-point and the stillness in the sphere's centre. Choose a topic you want to receive insights about. State your intention. Ask the sphere to activate itself and to show you insights and visions with respect to that topic. Close your eyes, feel the still energy of the sphere and be open to anything emerging from the sphere's depth in the form of an image, words, a feeling or a knowing.

CREATION OF YOUR HEART'S DESIRES:

Find a suitable (golden) sphere and hold it in your hands, perhaps rolling it around from time to time. Go into your zero-point and breathe. Connect with your sphere energetically by intention. Choose something you want to create from the deepest part of your being. State your intention in the present tense as if it is already a reality. Now use your emotions to amplify the intention of your thoughts. How would you feel if your creation already existed in your life? Hold those feelings and the corresponding body sensations. Ask the sphere to activate itself and to support you in creating your heart's desires. Feel the energy of the sphere. Stay connected to your vision and heart's desire and hand over any doubts and attempts at controlling the process to your Higher Self. What shows up in the form of an image, words, a feeling or a knowing? Is there a step for you to take?

At the end of these practices, you may wish to thank the sphere for its support, write the insights down in a journal and plan any corresponding actions. If you record these practices, you can listen to your voice guiding you into these experiences while closing your eyes. I recommend connecting to the sphere whenever you want to receive insights or create your heart's desires.

**Dodecahedron and Hexahedron:**

**Step 1: Dodecahedron for insights about your heart's desires:**

The dodecahedron is a suitable geometric form to facilitate your connection to higher realms and to call in your inner wisdom and insights. It assists you in gaining clarity about which decisions are in alignment with your soul and with the highest outcome for all concerned.

Practices:

DECISIONS ALIGNED WITH YOUR SOUL AND THE HIGHEST OUTCOME FOR ALL CONCERNED:

Go into your zero-point. See, sense or feel a huge dodecahedron in front of you and energetically step into its centre by intention. Ask the dodecahedron to activate itself and to rotate around, within and through you with the intention of supporting you in taking decisions that are aligned with your soul and the highest and best good of all concerned. Relax into its energies.

Then formulate decisions as statements and see, sense, feel or know how expansive or contractive your heart chakra becomes while making the statements. An expansion in the heart chakra indicates that the decision is aligned with the highest and best good whereas a contraction in the heart chakra indicates that the decision is not similarly aligned. You might also feel an expansion or contraction in the cells of your body.

Examples of decision statements:

* "It is in the highest to accept job offer x."
* "It is in the highest to rent this apartment."
* "It is in the highest to take this one-year training course."

Do you feel an expansion or contraction in your heart chakra when making these statements?

If you are not sure about the outcome, you can make the opposite statement and tune into your heart chakra. Always start the statements from your neutral zero-point. Be aware that it might not be in your highest interest, or the right moment for you, to know the answer to your question. If you feel that might be the case, you can check with the following statement: "It is in the highest for me to know the answer to my question now (or: to take the decision now)." The answer might also change as time goes by so you might want to check in again at a later stage.

When you have some experience with this practice, you can also use this technique of tuning into the expansion or contraction of your heart chakra while making statements without first calling in the dodecahedron.

## ASKING FOR GUIDANCE AND INSIGHTS:

Go into your zero-point. Install a dodecahedron vortex or grid in your energy system by intention or meditate with a dodecahedron. Ask the dodecahedron vortex or grid to activate itself and to support you in connecting to your inner wisdom and in facilitating guidance and insights that are relevant to you at the present moment. Tune in: What information is coming through? Then ask for the insights to be anchored into your energy system.

Examples of insights I have received and anchored into my energy system:

* The universe has your back. Let go of fear.
* Life is happening FOR you, not TO you.
* Keep doing what presents in every moment rather than trying to figure out the future with your rational mind.

\*    The power of love is stronger than anything else (such as the love of power).

## Step 2: Hexahedron for bringing visions into form:

The form-giving attributes, the stability and the structure of a hexahedron assist you in bringing etheric energies into physical manifestation.

Practices:

MATERIALISING YOUR VISION OR HEART'S DESIRE:

Go into your zero-point. Write your vision – or your heart's desire – on a piece of paper. Be sure that your vision or desire is aligned with your heart and soul rather than being a product of your rational mind. This can be checked with the help of the first dodecahedron practice above. Place a physical hexahedron on top of that piece of paper or set the intention to place an etheric hexahedron around your vision or desire. Ask the hexahedron to activate itself and to support the materialisation of your vision or heart's desire.

GROUNDING HIGH VIBRATIONAL ENERGIES:

Go into your zero-point. Ask for the installation and activation of a hexahedron grid in and around a certain place or location with the intention of grounding high vibrational energies of light there for the highest and best good of all concerned. Tune into the energies of your chosen place: How does it feel?

## Visionary work with the pentagram/pentagon[27]

The pentagram is a perfect sacred geometry shape for visionary work as it facilitates insights from the perspective of your soul, your essence.

I invite you to work with the pentagram by looking at your vision, or an important question or topic you have, from different perspectives. Assign a different intelligence to each of the five points of the pentagram/pentagon as shown in Figure 84:

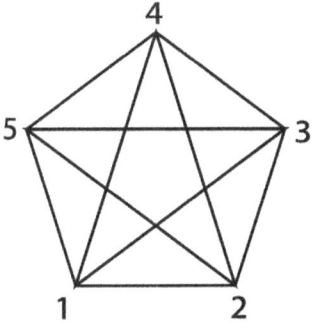

Figure 84: Visionary pentagram/pentagon

Let the five points of the pentagram/pentagon represent the following types of intelligence:

1. Structural intelligence – structure, rules, order
2. Emotional intelligence – feeling
3. Rational intelligence – action
4. Inspirational intelligence – concepts, ideas
5. Heart intelligence – heart's desires, wisdom of soul

You can work with the pentagram/pentagon in the following way on your own or accompanied by a partner or coach.

---

27  I was inspired to come up with this pentagram/pentagon practice by Dr. Hans Hein's work with the model of tetrahedral intelligences based on Buckminster Fuller's synergetics (see references to his work in Chapter 10).

* Go into your zero-point.
* Define your vision, topic or question, for example, "expansion of my business".
* Set up the above-mentioned five points with their related intelligences in the form of a pentagram/pentagon in your space. I recommend using your physical space and stepping onto each point physically but you can also draw a pentagram/pentagon on a piece of paper and mentally connect with each point.
* Starting with point number 1, step onto each point, feel into your vision, topic or question from that point's perspective and receive information through words, images, feelings, body sensations or a knowing. Record or write down the information. If you do this practice with a coach or partner, he or she can support you by asking questions and/or by feeling into the point as well to complement the information you receive.
* When you have received information on point number 1, move on to point number 2 and proceed as described in the last paragraph.
* Continue in chronological order through points 1 to 5. Each point will give you the information from the perspective of the intelligence related to that specific point. For instance, point 1 will give you the structural intelligence's perspective and inspire you to create specific structures or rules related to your topic, e.g. about your business expansion. At the end, you will have collected valuable inspirations from all five perspectives (structural, emotional, rational, inspirational and heart's desires) for your vision, topic or question.
* By stepping into the centre of the pentagram/pentagon at the end, meditate on the overall picture of the different pieces of the puzzle. Record or write down your insights.

You can also do the practice in the reverse order, starting with the heart intelligence (point 5) and moving on to the corresponding concepts (4), actions (3), feelings (2) and structures (1).

If you are familiar with constellations, you can introduce the pentagram/pentagon into your constellations, especially for visionary work. Choose five representatives, one for each intelligence, and let the representatives share their insights. At the end, step into the centre of the pentagram/pentagon and experience the shared insights.

## Manifesting your heart's desires with the five Platonic solids

Instead of – or in addition to – working with the pentagram/pentagon as described above, you can use the five Platonic solids and their related elements. Each Platonic solid then represents one of the five intelligences mentioned above and contributes its specific energies and elemental connections to one of the five perspectives. In detail:

1: Structural intelligence — structure, rules, order   Hexahedron, earth element

2: Emotional intelligence – feeling   Icosahedron, water element

3: Rational intelligence – action   Tetrahedron, fire element

4: Inspirational intelligence — concepts, ideas   Octahedron, air element

5: Heart intelligence — heart's desires, wisdom of soul   Dodecahedron, ether element

Here is a suggestion for the process:
* Go into your zero-point.
* Choose a specific heart's desire or "heart's desires" as a general topic.
* Set the intention to allocate the various types of intelligence to the respective Platonic solids, as described above.
* Starting with intelligence number 1, connect to the hexahedron in one of the ways described in Chapter 6. I recommend meditating with a physical representation or a printout version of the Platonic solid and/or energetically inviting the Platonic solid into your body and energetic system.
* As suggested above, connect to the hexahedron, meditate with it and/or invite it into your body and energetic system. Ask it to activate itself and start rotating within, around and through you with the intention of supporting you with your heart's

desire(s) from its related intelligence perspective, in this case the perspective of structural intelligence. Ask the hexahedron and the corresponding element of earth for structural support in materialising your heart's desire(s). Close your eyes, if you wish to. You might see images, hear words or sounds, feel or sense energy (shifts) and/or receive an insight. If nothing comes to you, don't worry and try again later.

* Continue with the next intelligence and the corresponding Platonic solid and element in the chronological order described above. Next connect with the icosahedron, meditate with it and/or invite it into your body and energetic system. Ask it to activate itself and start rotating within, around and through you with the intention of supporting you with your heart's desire(s) from the perspective of emotional intelligence. Ask the icosahedron and the corresponding element of water for emotional support in materialising your heart's desire(s) and watch what emerges. Continue with numbers 3, 4 and 5 in the same way.

* At the end of the five rounds, go into your zero-point and tune into your overall experience. You might want to hand the manifestation of your heart's desire(s) in cosmic timing over to your Higher Self.

The practice may also be conducted in the reverse order, starting with the heart intelligence (point 5) and moving on to the corresponding concepts (4), actions (3), feelings (2) and structures (1).

Let me summarise my own experiences as follows:

In the visionary work with the pentagram/pentagon constellation, many new insights and inspirations regarding my topic emerged. During the Platonic solid practice with my heart's desires, I experienced many energy shifts and received activations of my multidimensional DNA and inner wisdom.

## 7.11
## From Feeling Out of Flow to Aligning with Natural and Cosmic Rhythms

**7-pointed star:**

The 7-pointed star supports you in regaining balance and harmony within and with the elements around you. It reflects the cyclical attributes and inherent rhythms of creation, nature and the cosmos. These are reflected in the 7 days of creation, the 7 days of the week, the 7 main chakras of the human body and the 7 universal laws, for example.

Choose the version of a 7-pointed star that most appeals to you and your topic (see Chapter 5.3 for examples) – or create your own version! Connect with its energy. In the following paragraphs you will find some general practices to help you return to your natural flow.

You can work with the 7-pointed star when you have lost your natural balance and flow in order to return to harmony and alignment with your body and organic life, or invite it in whenever you are in survival mode and pushing to try to make things happen. Returning to being "natural" means relaxing into your true nature and feeling inherently valuable and worthy. It's an invitation to be fully conscious that you are part of everything and everything is part of you and that there is no need to be living in survival mode. Instead, it's time to blossom and thrive!

Practices:

RETURNING TO HARMONY WITH YOUR BODY:

Go into your zero-point. Tune into your body and invite a 7-pointed star (vortex) into your energetic system. Ask it to activate itself, rotate and spin in all directions to support your body in regaining its natural rhythm and flow. Ask your body for any messages that might further support this process.

I also invite you to place a printout version of a 7-pointed star on certain body parts over night or when asking the 7-pointed star to help you activate your natural flow.

## CONNECTING WITH NATURE AND THE COSMOS:

You might want to choose the 7-pointed Fairy Star for this practice. Go into your zero-point and breathe. Energetically – by intention – step into a 7-pointed star that is right in front of you and see, sense or feel how it expands in all directions. Ask it to activate itself and rotate around and through you with the intention of strengthening your connection with nature and the cosmos. See, sense, feel or know that you are in flow with all life and aligned with natural and cosmic cycles and rhythms. Nothing in nature and the cosmos questions its inherent value or purpose. Relax into your true nature. It is time to blossom and thrive!

## ADVANCING IN AN ORGANIC WAY:

Constant change – happening in cycles – is part of the human experience. I invite you to experience the 7-pointed star multidimensionally in the form of a spiral rather than as a continuous wheel of life. You may choose either the 7-pointed Fairy Star or the 7-pointed Hermetic Principles Star for this practice.

Go into your zero-point. I invite you to close your eyes. By intention step into a multidimensional 7-pointed star in front of you and see, sense or feel how it expands in all directions. See, sense, feel or know that you are in flow with all life. Set the intention to move upwards in line with natural and cosmic cycles and laws. Ask the 7-pointed star to activate itself and to support you in your endeavour through its movements and frequencies. See, sense, feel or know that you are spiralling upwards, thus advancing in alignment with nature and the cosmos. Experience a new, higher vibrational level on each turn of the spiral while going through the cycles, supported by your conscious breathing. You are advancing in an organic way.

**Pyramid:**

The pyramid assists you in connecting to the cosmos and Earth and in improving energy flow within you. As a vehicle of transformation, the pyramid also facilitates alchemical processes within you.

Practices:

REVITALISING YOUR ENERGY FLOW IN ALIGNMENT WITH THE COSMOS AND EARTH:

Go into your zero-point. Call for a golden pyramid to come down over you, the base of which is at navel height and with its peak about 45 cm or 18 inches above your crown (at the tip of your upwards stretched arms and hands). Relax into its golden frequency. Energetically connect to the peak of the pyramid above you and, using your imagination and your breath, invite a stream of golden-white light from the cosmos down into the pyramid and your energetic system for your highest and best good. Connect with the cosmos as you inhale and exhale.

Now call for another golden pyramid to come up from underneath you, which is a mirror image of the first pyramid and whose base connects to the first pyramid's base at the height of your navel. Its peak stretches down to a point just below your feet. Relax into its golden frequency. Energetically connect to the peak of the pyramid below you pointing towards Earth and, using your imagination and your breath, invite a stream of golden-white light from Inner Earth up into the pyramid and your energetic system for your highest and best good. Connect with the Earth through your inhalation and your exhalation.

When you feel connected with the cosmos and the Earth, ask the golden-white energies of the two pyramids – which are connected to form an octahedron – to flow into every cell of your body and to assist you in revitalising your energy flow. Breathe and relax into the renewed energy flow.

## REGENERATION AND REJUVENATION OF YOUR BODY:

Go into your zero-point. Call for a pyramid of alchemy to come down over you whose base is at the height of your navel and whose peak is about 45 cm or 18 inches above your crown (at the tip of your upwards stretched arms and hands). Does the pyramid have a specific colour or tone to it? Relax into its alchemical frequency. Now call for another pyramid of alchemy to come up from underneath you, which is a mirror image of the first pyramid and whose base connects to the first pyramid's base at the height of your navel. Its peak stretches down to a point just below your feet. Does this pyramid have a specific colour or tone to it? Relax into its alchemical frequency. Using your imagination and your breath, connect to the peak of the first pyramid above you and the peak of the second pyramid below you. See, sense or feel yourself inside of this octahedral structure.

When you feel connected to the cosmos and the Earth, invite the two pyramids to activate themselves and to start the process of alchemy within your body and energy system, supporting all cells in your body in regenerating, rejuvenating and regaining their natural vitality. The pyramids might want to rotate or spin. Let any colours, tones and/or movements emerge, which further support the process. Breathe and relax into the alchemical process. Are you feeling revitalised now?

## 7.12
# Expanding from Your Rational Mind into Universal Intelligence and Wisdom

Figure 85: 8-pointed star design

**8-pointed star:**

The 8-pointed star supports you in expanding your consciousness and creativity and helps you put it into practice in your life. Using the 8-pointed star with a specific intention might facilitate stronger energy shifts and a more focused impact in line with your intention.

Practices:

EXPANDING YOUR CONSCIOUSNESS AND STRENGTH-ENING YOUR INTUITION:

Go into your zero-point. Step into a physical 8-pointed star on the ground, or imagine an 8-pointed star in front of you and energetically step into its centre by intention. Call for the activation of the 8-pointed star and experience its energy. Ask the 8-pointed star to rotate for your highest and best good. The two squares might rotate in different directions or not. You might see the star in certain colours or not. Just be in the experience. Now invite the energy of the 8-pointed star into your energy system. Invite the star to dance within you.

Or you might prefer to imagine yourself dancing in or with the star. Just follow your intuition. Play with the 8-pointed star. Observe: Are there energy shifts in your body? What are your bodily sensations? Do emotions, thoughts or insights come up? Intuitively go with what emerges. Your body might want to move or make sounds. Enjoy the experience. Ask the 8-pointed star to support you in expanding your consciousness and in strengthening your intuition. See, sense or feel the expansiveness in your energetic system.

## SHARING YOUR EXPANDED CONSCIOUSNESS WITH THE WORLD:

Go into your zero-point. Imagine an 8-pointed star in front of you and step into its centre by intention. Call for the activation of the 8-pointed star and feel its energy. Breathe into it to make it stronger. See, sense or feel how your energetic system expands. Let the expansion increase with the help of your breath and focused awareness. Then set the intention to emanate your expanded consciousness out into the world, like planting seeds of love. You may wish to visualise a blow ball from a dandelion sharing its seeds of love with the world through the wind, or the Sun radiating out its rays onto Earth and its inhabitants. Do you perceive an expansion in your heart chakra?

**Flower of Life:**

The Flower of Life supports you in remembering your divine origin.

Practices:

## UNIVERSAL CONNECTION:

Go into your zero-point. Through your intention, breath and focus see, sense or feel the connection of the Flower of Life in your heart chakra with the Flower of Life in the centre of the Earth and with the Flower of Life in the centre of our Sun. Ask the Flowers of Life for a stronger connection with one another. What do you perceive?

RETURNING HOME:

Go into your zero-point. See, sense or feel a multidimensional unbounded Flower of Life in front of you. Energetically step into the centre of one of its spheres and ask for the activation of the Flower of Life. Set the intention to call all your energies – which are now ready to return – back from all timelines, dimensions, planes, aspects, realities and bodies cleansed and purified through your zero-point into your cellular body, into the here and now. Relax into the present moment and your true nature and breathe slowly and deeply. Claim your divine blueprint. Experience how your energy and life force return to your heart chakra, to the centre of your own Flower of Life within you and from there on into your cellular body.

# 7.13
# From Duality and Fragmentation to Interconnectedness and Wholeness

**Vesica Piscis:**

The Vesica Piscis symbolises duality and balance and plays an important part in the evolution of consciousness from creation to the experience of duality and back to wholeness/oneness. It can be used to reflect on and shift your experiences of polarities in your life and relationships.

You can do the Vesica Piscis practices energetically, as described below, or intuitively create a physical Vesica Piscis with stones, crystals, ropes, round pieces of paper or drawings for you to step into or reflect upon while going through the practices.

Practice:

REFLECTION OF YOUR CURRENT EXPERIENCE OF OPPOSITES:

Go into your zero-point. Choose the opposites you want to explore. Examples of polarities are: two individuals in a romantic or business partnership or in general; your human self and your Higher Self (where the heart chakra could serve as the centre of the intersection area); the masculine and the feminine within you; the outer world and the inner world. Define which circle represents which polarity.

Meditate with the Vesica Piscis. Ask it to show you through the sizes and shapes of its two circles and their intersection how you are currently experiencing these polarities in your life.

Reflect on what you see, sense, feel or know:

*   What do the sizes and the shapes of the circles tell you? Are they of equal size?
*   How big is the intersection? Does it feel or look harmonious?
*   Do you see colours or hear tones?

Take your time to explore the meaning of what you perceive.

Taking the example of a partnership, the image of a Vesica Piscis with two whole, complete and equal (in size and shape) circles with a large and vibrant intersection could symbolise two partners who know themselves as equal and who experience their union vibrantly, while remaining whole and complete on their own.

SHIFT IN YOUR PERSPECTIVE OF OPPOSITES:

Go into your zero-point. Choose the opposites you want to explore and allocate a circle to each polarity. Step into the first circle and experience the opposites from that perspective. Then shift your perspective by stepping from this circle into the intersection of the two circles. Which sensations, thoughts, emotions or insights do you perceive? What has changed?

You might also want to explore stepping into the second (other) circle and experiencing the opposites from that perspective. If the first circle represents you and the second circle another person, perceive how that other person is feeling with regard to your energy and actions coming from the first circle. How does that change your perception of your relationship and the other person?

SHIFT IN YOUR EXPERIENCE OF OPPOSITES:

Go into your zero-point. Choose the polarities you want to explore. Meditate with the Vesica Piscis. Ask it to show you through the sizes and shapes of its two circles and their intersection how you are currently experiencing those polarities in your life (see first practice). By intention, shift the circles energetically (and/or physically) to where you want them to be for the highest and best good of all concerned. Be aware of any emerging sensations, thoughts, emotions or insights. Step into the intersection and experience the polarities from that union of the two circles. How does it feel? You might also want to explore stepping into an outer circle. What changes now?

I had the following experience in a meditation with the Vesica Piscis on the relationship between my human self and Higher Self in 2016. I saw two fairly independent circles with a small intersection only. I stepped into the circle representing my Higher Self. I felt an expansion in my energy system and a strong connection with my creativity. I then moved over to the circle representing my human self. I felt the separation of my human self from my Higher Self through anger, frustration and even some despair. I noticed that my human self perceived life as a struggle. I then visualised the gradual merging of the two circles of the Vesica Piscis with the subsequent amplification of their intersection area and energetically stepped into the intersection. By choosing to step out of my perceived victimhood and separation into my creativity and a sense of wholeness, I felt empowered again.

**Trinity/Triad – Introducing the third circle and the third entity:**

The trinity or triad allows you to explore and shift the relationship between three beings, systems or energy fields such as the relationship between your body, mind and spirit or the co-creation of a third entity (e.g. a project) by two (business) partners.

Practice:

EXPLORATION OF, AND SHIFT IN, TRIAD RELATIONSHIPS:

Go into your zero-point. Choose the trinity you want to explore. Define which circle represents which being, system or energy field. You might first want to do the above-mentioned three Vesica Piscis practices with polarities. Then invite the third entity to join the opposites by adding a third circle representing the third entity energetically and/or physically (see Figure 16). Explore its shape, size and location. Which sensations, thoughts, emotions and/or insights come up? Step into the intersection of all three circles and experience the common area of the trinity. You can also explore the trinity from all possible perspectives and shift its circles energetically as described in the Vesica Piscis practices of opposites above.

**6-pointed star and 8-pointed star:**

The 6-pointed star supports you in centring yourself and harmonising polarities within you, while the 8-pointed star supports you in integrating internal polarities.

Practices:

HARMONISING POLARITIES WITHIN YOU:

Go into your zero-point. Invite a 6-pointed star vortex into your energy field by intention. See, sense or feel how the downward-pointing triangle connects you to the Earth below and the upward-pointing triangle to the Sun above. Breathe into your centre and relax into it. Now ask the 6-pointed star vortex to activate itself and rotate within your energy field with the intention of harmonising polarities within you. See, sense, feel or know how any fragmented aspects in your energy body return to harmony.

INTEGRATING POLARITIES WITHIN YOU:

Go into your zero-point. Invite an 8-pointed star vortex into your energy field by intention. Ask the 8-pointed star vortex to activate itself and rotate within your energy field with the intention of integrating polarities within you – for example, your male and female aspects. Relax, breathe and experience the vortex until it eventually slows down and comes to a standstill. Now see, sense, feel or know how the two opposing squares of the 8-pointed star have come together in one harmonious pattern and that the polarities within you have been integrated.

**Diamond:**

The diamond acts like a mirror: You see yourself in another. It also reflects your projections onto the outside world. By becoming aware of your projections and taking them back through a change in perspective and self-responsibility ("owning your creations"), you embark on the path from fragmentation to wholeness.

Practice:

BECOMING AWARE OF, AND OWNING, YOUR PROJECTIONS:

Go into your zero-point. You might want to close your eyes. See, sense or feel a diamond in front of you. Step inside by intention and ask the diamond to activate itself as a mirror for you. From the inside, look at the different facets of the world around you that the diamond is reflecting back to you. These are your projections from your inner to your outer world. Which facets of yours do you see reflected in your surroundings? Ask the diamond to spin and share its crystalline frequencies with you with the intention of taking back your projections and owning your creations. Breathe through this process until the diamond stops spinning. Breathe deeply and return to your inner centre. Then ask yourself: "Which reflections would I like to see? Which focus would serve that? Which frequency would bring that about?" Invite the corresponding frequencies and experiences in. Now tune into the reflections of the diamond around you: Do you perceive any changes?

# 7.14
# Discovering New Horizons and Universes Inside and Outside of You

**Merkaba:**

The Merkaba is a wonderful vehicle for travelling to other dimensions, realities and planes of existence to explore and receive information and insights.

During my travels within my Merkaba, I have experienced it slowly spinning like a celestial being.

Practice:

LIGHT BODY TRAVEL IN YOUR MERKABA:

First activate your personal Merkaba as described in Chapter 4.7. Now set the intention to travel in your light body for your highest and best good. You might want to specify where you want to go, for example a specific star system or planet. Set an intention of why you want to go on this journey. You might wish to explore a certain star or planet and have experiences that would assist you – and others – in your present life. Perhaps you'd like to receive insights, light codes and activations? If you want to consciously remember your experience, set this intention, too. Then engage in a meditation or stillness practice without expectation while remaining open to what is revealed either during the practice or in the following days.

**Diamond:**

The diamond is a suitable geometric form to connect with galactic and angelic realms and to activate your multidimensional facets and abilities such as clairvoyance and telepathic communication.

Practice:

## CONNECTING WITH THE STARS AND ACTIVATING MULTIDIMENSIONAL ABILITIES:

You might want to travel in your personal Merkaba to the centre of the universe first (see previous practice). Go into your zero-point. Set the intention to connect to your galactic chakra above your crown and to your multidimensional aspects. By intention see, sense or feel yourself inside a huge diamond in the centre of the universe, noticing or imagining how the crystalline qualities of the diamond reflect the light of the galaxies back to you. Tune in: Which (rainbow) light bridge to which star system or galaxy are you building? Ask the diamond to activate itself and spin within, around and through you with the intention of activating the multidimensional abilities of your DNA. Tune in again: Which of your multidimensional abilities are being activated right now? Who – on Earth and in the higher realms – is on your team to co-create with you?

Please also refer to Chapter 7.15 f) for building bridges to other people, dimensions and star systems with the Rainbow Ankh.

## 7.15
## Opening Doors with the Key of Life –
## the Egyptian Ankh

**The Ankh in general:**

The Ankh represents the key of (eternal) life – in all timelines, dimensions and realities. Experience this key of life in your own body and energy system. Open the doors to higher realms and new realities with the Ankh. Assist people with depression or suicidal tendencies in choosing life.

Practices:

YOUR BODY AS THE HOLY GRAIL:

Go into your zero-point. Invite a golden Ankh to flow down from above into your crown chakra, on to your pineal gland near the centre of your brain behind the third eye and then on to your pituitary gland at the base of your brain. Ask the Ankh to activate itself and rotate in both glands with the intention of clearing and upgrading your glands. After a while, invite the golden Ankh to flow down through your throat into the centre of your heart chakra. From there see, sense or feel how the Ankh expands, allowing you to embody the golden Ankh: Its oval loop moves to the back of your head, the horizontal line of the Ankh flows into your outstretched arms and its vertical line flows down your lower chakras into your feet, connecting with the Earth. Tune into the experience of your body as the golden Ankh, as the Holy Grail for your essence. You might want to ask your golden body Ankh to move or spin with the intention of increasing your life force. Breathe through the process.

SUPPORTING PEOPLE WITH DEPRESSION AND SUICIDAL TENDENCIES:

Here are some recommendations on how to support people with depression and suicidal tendencies:

- Invite this person to meditate with the Ankh symbol.
- Hand them a physical Ankh, inviting them to wear it around their necks or to use it as a decorative item in their homes.
- Inspire them to create their own Ankh through a drawing, a painting or forming it with clay, crystals or stones.
- With their consent – if you cannot ask the person directly, ask his or her Higher Self for permission – energetically work with the Burning Ankh to clear their energetic systems and then, with the Illuminated Ankh, to light up the person (see practices b) and e) listed below) or with any type of Ankh that presents itself.
- With the other person's consent – if you cannot ask the person directly, ask his or her Higher Self for permission – invite a golden Ankh into their auric fields, asking it to activate itself and rotate with the intention of repairing, healing and sealing off any holes in the auric fields for their highest and best good.

**Different aspects of the Ankh**

Enjoy the various aspects of the Ankh, which Isis showed me for the purposes described below.

Introduction to different ways of working with the Ankh:

- You can do the practices as described below for your whole energy system. Alternatively, let the Ankh rotate and spin in certain parts of your physical body and/or energy body to clear and shift energy in specific areas connected to your physical body, emotions, belief systems or your energetic field.
- You can activate the Ankh from within, or allow it into your energy system from elsewhere, for example from above or below.

I have used different ways of activation for the practices described below, as I felt guided. Please feel free to invite the Ankh into your energy field in the way that most resonates with you.

- Ask the Ankh to move, rotate, spin and tilt in alignment with your highest and best good.

- You can put a physical Ankh, or a printed image of one, on different parts of your body, for example at night. I experienced a powerful transformation process related to a specific body part by doing this. It was particularly strong when I placed the Ankh image on my back and on the back of my chakras.

- You can pick and play with one or several versions of the Ankh, or use the various practices displaying different qualities of the Ankh in the sequence described below, starting with the Upside-Down Ankh and proceeding in chronological order from a) to f).

### a) The Upside-Down Ankh: facilitating a deeper connection to Earth

Figure 86: Upside-Down Ankh

Background: The Ankh is supportive in connecting to the cosmos as well as to the Earth. When you turn the Ankh to face downwards, it facilitates a stronger connection to Earth.

Practice:

Connect to the Upside-Down Ankh (see Figure 86) from your zero-point and activate it for your highest and best good. Set the intention to build a stronger connection to Earth. See, sense or feel how the oval loop of the Upside-Down Ankh connects to, and wraps itself around, the crystal heart of the Earth. Breathe the crystalline energy from the Earth's heart up through your feet into your energy system. See, sense or feel a flow of crystalline energy going up through your body into your outstretched arms – the Ankh's horizontal line – and further upwards through your head – the Upside-Down Ankh's "feet" – out into the universe.

Now I invite you to imagine little Upside-Down Ankhs going downwards from your zero-point into the Earth to anchor you onto planet Earth through the key of (earthly) life while little "Upright Ankhs" (see Figure 41) are going upwards from your zero-point, connecting you to the cosmos through the key of eternal life. You might want to use your breath to strengthen your connection to the Earth's core below and to the cosmos above: Breathe crystalline and luminous white energy from the Earth into you, up and out and then from the cosmos into you, down and out. We are connected to the heavens above and the Earth below, being part of both the cosmos and the Earth.

### b) The Burning Ankh: destroying old energies and limitations

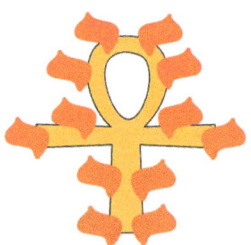

Figure 87: Burning Ankh

Background: The well-intended power of destruction allows for the required change for evolution and growth on individual and collective levels. When you hand over an old thought, pattern or conditioning to sacred flames of destruction, a higher vibrational energy form can emerge, enhancing your experience of freedom.

Practice:

Connect to the Ankh from your zero-point in the middle of your heart chakra. Invite the Burning Ankh (see Figure 87) into your energy system for your highest and best good. Set the intention to destroy old energies, limiting patterns and belief systems that no longer serve you. Ask the Burning Ankh to activate itself and rotate in your energy system to assist you in destroying these old energies, belief systems and limitations. See, sense or feel how belief systems, patterns and limitations within you are set on fire, how walls come tumbling down, and how imperfections within your energy field are purified in the sacred flames of destruction. Breathe and relax into the energies. See, sense or feel how, after a while, the spin of the Ankh slows down, revealing to you an opening and a new awareness. Rise from the ashes like a phoenix ready to experience the potential and expansion of new beginnings.

c) **The Kundalini Ankh: activating the heart chakra, life force and kundalini energy**

Figure 88: Kundalini Ankh

Background: A Kundalini Ankh emerges out of two individual Ankhs: Put two Ankhs together on top of one another, with one Ankh facing upwards towards the Sun and the other facing downwards towards the Earth, merging with each other in the heart chakra and the outstretched arms. The overall image is similar to an equilateral cross with two oval loops at the top and bottom of the vertical line or an upright infinity symbol with outstretched arms. When two become one, infinity reveals itself.

The Kundalini Ankh displays energetic qualities which are similar to two Kundalini serpents moving up the chakras in an interweaving thread-and-needle principle.

Practice:

Connect to the Kundalini Ankh (see Figure 88) from your zero-point and call for its activation. Invite the two Ankhs that form the Kundalini Ankh to go up your spine through the chakras in an interweaving thread-and-needle pattern. You might see, sense or feel two energies going upwards at the left and right sides of your spine while interconnecting with each other on your spine at the heights of your chakras. When the Ankhs reach the top of your head, ask the downward-facing Ankh to go straight down again to your feet while the other Ankh stays at the top of your head pointing towards the Sun. See, sense or feel how both Ankhs come together in your heart chakra and your outstretched arms. Ask the Kundalini Ankh to activate itself and to spin, move and rotate in your body and energy system for your highest and best good, with the intention of activating the life force and kundalini energy within you. Breathe deeply. Do you feel an activation of your heart chakra?

**d) The Golden-White Ankh with rays of violet, gold and diamond white light: supporting transmutation, purification and activation of the essence within you**

Figure 89: Golden-White Ankh

Background: The Golden-White Ankh with rays of violet, gold and diamond white light was offered to me by Isis to support you with transmutation, purification and the activation of the essence within you. The various rays of light come in for different purposes. They work simultaneously, rotating and emanating their specific codes into your energy system. The violet ray assists with transmutation. The golden ray supports you in purifying the physical body and mind, freeing them of old paradigms so that you can embody the highest light and potential possible at every moment. The diamond white ray enhances your luminosity and purity and activates the essence within you. The Golden-White Ankh supports you in your authenticity, in being truly you.

Practice:

Connect to the Golden-White Ankh (see Figure 89) from your zero-point and ask for its activation with rays of violet, gold and diamond white light. Invite it into your body, mind and energy system, asking it to rotate from your zero-point in the middle of your heart chakra for your highest and best good. See, sense or feel how rays of violet, gold and diamond white light pour out of your zero-point, noticing how the moving Ankh emanates these colour codes into every cell of your physical body and into your mind and energy system. See, sense or feel how the violet ray assists with transmutation of the old and how the golden ray purifies your physical body and mind and clears old paradigms from your energy system. See, sense or feel how the diamond white light enhances your luminosity and purity and activates your essence. Notice how the energies and codes of this Golden-White Ankh go deeper and deeper into your body, mind and energy system while spreading the rays of light into every cell, infusing the chakras and organs, going deeper and wider until your whole being is lit up in a golden-white light. Feel or know that you are completely renewed. See, sense or feel yourself as the embodiment of the highest light and potential possible for you in this moment.

## e) The Illuminated Ankh: spreading grace and universal love

Figure 90: Illuminated Ankh

Background: In every moment and in every situation in your life the power of grace and universal love creates the opportunity for peace, new openings, expansion and the experience of fulfilment. The power of grace literally creates each moment with the intention of awakening you to who you really are. The power of universal love allows you to realise that you ARE love and supports you in embodying that expression in the world.

Practices:

## Version 1: Activating the Illuminated Ankh from within

I invite you to let your body form an Ankh by standing up straight, stretching out your arms to both sides and moving your legs close together. Connect to the Illuminated Ankh (see Figure 90) and by intention activate it from your zero-point in the middle of your heart chakra. See, sense or feel how luminous energy flows from your zero-point into the back of your head and all around your head – this movement represents the oval loop of the Ankh – and from there into both outstretched arms, then from your zero-point in the heart chakra down into your torso, your lower chakras and into your feet. See, sense or feel how the luminous energy of the Illuminated Ankh flows into every cell of your body, into your physical body, your emotions, your thoughts and beliefs and your whole energetic system. See, sense or feel how your whole being is completely illuminated. Ask the Illuminated Ankh to rotate in your energy system with the intention of expanding and spreading the luminous energy to every cell – down to the quantum level. Your body might want to make movements or it might want to stand still. See, sense or feel yourself as a being of light. Breathe deeply.

**Version 2: Inviting the Illuminated Ankh into your energy field**

Connect to the Illuminated Ankh (see Figure 90) from your zero-point in the middle of your heart chakra, inviting it into your body and energy field from above through your crown. Ask it to activate itself, spin and share its light for your highest and best good. See, sense or feel how an Illuminated Ankh in a white, luminescent light enters your body and energy system through your crown chakra. Breathe deeply. See, sense or feel how this Illuminated Ankh slides deeper and deeper into your body and energy system while spinning and spreading the energy of grace and universal love into every cell of your body and energy field, going down through your body and your chakras, deeper and deeper, until your whole being is lit up. See, sense or feel how your body has become the Illuminated Ankh and you a being of radiant light.

**f) The Rainbow Ankh: building bridges to other people, dimensions and star systems**

Figure 91: Rainbow Ankh

229

Background: The crystalline qualities of the Rainbow Ankh reflect diffcrent vibrational facets of you. You can connect to your multidimensional nature and experience other people, dimensions and star systems by connecting with the different colours of the Rainbow Ankh.

Practice:

Connect to the Rainbow Ankh (see Figure 91) from your zero-point and ask it to activate itself and reflect your multidimensional aspects back to you. Set the intention to build a connecting bridge to someone or something, for instance to other people, dimensions or star systems, for the highest and best good of all concerned. Ask the Rainbow Ankh to spread out its light from your zero-point to the people, dimensions or star systems you have requested to connect to. See, sense or feel how the light – it could be (a) specific colour(s) or the whole rainbow spectrum – builds a bridge to the other person or realm. Invite the connection to grow stronger. Experience the connection to, and interaction with, the other person or realm. Breathe and relax into this experience. You might want to ask questions. See, sense or feel how this connection enriches you and how it expands your multidimensional facets and consciousness. At the end you may choose to imagine yourself radiating the rainbow colours into your surroundings.

**The Rainbow Ankh in a Heart: supporting loved ones on their way into another dimension/life**

Figure 92: Rainbow Ankh in a Heart

Background: The Rainbow Ankh in a Heart is composed of the Ankh, the rainbow colours and the symbol of the heart. The Ankh is a key to eternal life and opens up other dimensions. The rainbow colours facilitate a shift in one's energy and vibration to go from one dimension/realm to another, for instance in the moment of passing. This process is embedded in the heart, symbolising universal love and the love you have for that person.

Practice:

You might choose to show a colour image of the Rainbow Ankh in a Heart (see Figure 92) to the person who is ready to pass on to another dimension of light before initiating the following process: When the time has come for a soul to leave its earthly body to go home, connect to the Rainbow Ankh in a Heart from your zero-point. Also connect to the zero-point of the person who is ready to transition. You might see, sense or feel a rainbow bridge from your zero-point to theirs. Ask for the Rainbow Ankh in a Heart to be activated and offer it as the key to eternal life to the other person's soul. This will help the soul's journey home in love with ease and grace. If you see, sense, feel or know that there are still energetic cords between you and the loved one that are holding them back on Earth and that do not serve you anymore, ask for your guides and angels to cut the cords for the highest and best good of all concerned. Feel the love, rather than a loss.

# 7.16
# Playing with Your Infinite Nature
# Through the Infinity Symbol

Figure 93: Blueberry infinity symbol

The infinity symbol assists you with the following:

- Restoring balance
- Cutting cords and disposing of old and/or foreign energies
- Full-circling, completing and integrating experiences
- Finding inner peace and accessing the power of NOW
- Accessing the quantum field, experiencing oneness and creating new experiences

Practices:

You can do all the practices below energetically by setting an intention and using your imagination. Some of the practices would work well with a physical infinity symbol that you create on the ground in front of you.

RESTORING BALANCE:

Go into your zero-point. Imagine an infinity symbol connecting certain body parts for balance. To support your imagination, you can trace the infinity symbol with your fingers or by breathing into the movement. Feel the centre of the infinity symbol at the point where its two loops come together. Examples for body parts to be connected are as follows: left hemisphere of the brain to right hemisphere of the brain (centre: pineal gland behind your third eye); heart chakra to third eye (centre: throat chakra); left ovary to right ovary (centre: womb); feet to crown chakra (centre: groin); centre of the Earth to centre of our Sun (centre: your heart chakra).

If you want to repeat this practice, you can record a guided meditation for yourself, taking you from one body part to the next.

BALANCING AND FULL-CIRCLING OPPOSITE EXPERIENCES:

Choose your opposite experiences. To give you an example, imagine that you sometimes experience having lots of money, spending lots of money, feeling abundant and being generous whereas at other times you experience lack of money, going into debt, feeling financially insecure and being stingy. Another example is feeling inferior versus feeling superior at times.

Go into your zero-point. See, sense or feel a horizontal infinity symbol (∞) in front of you. You might want to create a physical infinity symbol with a rope or a thread on the ground in front of you. By intention energetically place into the infinity symbol's first loop all your experiences of one extreme, e.g. all your experiences of wealth and abundance. Then place into the infinity symbol's second loop all your experiences of the opposite extreme, e.g. all your experiences of lack and poverty. Step physically or energetically into the intersection of the infinity symbol in front of you with the two loops to the left and right sides of you. Tune into both extremes simultaneously and feel their frequencies. When you are ready, gather the two opposite loops of the infinity symbol from the ground – or set the intention of doing so – and collapse them into one circle rising vertically out of the intersection. See, sense or feel how the opposite experiences merge into one, balancing each other out. Feel or sense the re-set in your experiences, or know that your opposite experiences have come full circle.

CUTTING CORDS AND DISPOSING OF OLD AND/OR
FOREIGN ENERGIES:

You can do this practice with energies in your energetic system that
do not belong to you and/or do not serve you anymore either in
general or related to a specific person, topic or area of experience
such as health, finance, relationships.

Go into your zero-point. Choose the person, topic or area of experience
you want to work with or invite any experience in. Imagine a vertical
infinity symbol (8) in front of you. Step into one of its two loops.
Set the intention to place all the topic-related energies that do not
belong to you and/or all that no longer serve you from your energetic
system into the second loop of the infinity symbol, outside the one
you are standing in. See, sense or feel yourself in one loop and the
foreign and/or old energies in the other loop. Breathe. When you
feel the moment has come, ask your Higher Self to cut the figure 8
of the infinity symbol into two halves, taking care of the energies in
the outside loop. See, sense or feel how the outside half dissolves or
disappears until all that is left is you inside your circle.[28]

FULL-CIRCLING THE OLD AND STEPPING INTO THE NEW:

You can do this practice with energies in your energetic system that do
not belong to you and/or do not serve you anymore either generally
or in relation to a specific person, topic or area of experience such as
health, finance and relationships.

Go into your zero-point and breathe. See, sense or feel a vertical
infinity symbol in front of you – like the number "8" – or create one
on the ground. Step into its centre, the intersection of the two loops,
energetically or physically, and look ahead. By intention place all the
topic-related old patterns and energies that are not yours and/or that

---

[28] For a thorough method to cut cords with a person or a pattern check out Phyllis
Krystal's method at https://www.phylliskrystal.com/method/#start.

do not serve you anymore from your energetic system into the loop of the infinity symbol behind you. Place your (topic-related) heart's desires and projects as fresh energies into the loop in front of you. From your present place, feel the old and foreign energies behind you and the new energies in front of you. Breathe. When you feel the moment has come, declare that you are ready to full-circle the old and step into the new. Step into the loop ahead of you into new beginnings. Ask your Higher Self to cut off the loop behind you. See, sense or feel how that loop dissolves until all that is left is you inside the circle of new beginnings. Enjoy your new life!

This practice is very helpful when you are starting a new project or phase in your life.

LEAVING A TREADMILL:

Go into your zero-point. See, sense or feel the situation where you're feeling stuck ("treadmill") as a constant loop reflected in an infinity symbol. Take a decision to leave this treadmill. See, sense or feel how new infinity symbols emerge that all intersect at one point. Energetically step into this intersection point of all infinity symbols and choose a new infinity symbol that represents a higher level of consciousness for you. Set the intention to jump from the old infinity symbol (the "treadmill") to this new one of higher vibrations. See, sense or feel how you land in this new infinity symbol while the others dissolve. See, sense or feel yourself in this new reality.

COLLECTING YOUR ASPECTS AND INTEGRATING EXPERIENCES:

Go into your zero-point. See, sense or feel a huge infinity symbol going up from the centre of the Earth to the Sun above with its intersection located in your zero-point in the middle of your heart chakra. Relax into your zero-point where the opposite loops of the figure "8" co-exist in absolute equilibrium with each other until you feel or know yourself beyond time and space. Ask the infinity symbol to activate itself and to rotate through all timelines, dimensions, planes of existence and realities with the intention of collecting and retrieving all your aspects – that are ready to return – cleansed and purified back into your zero-point. Breathe and allow for the integration of your soul's experiences.

This practice can be done in general or for a specific topic, for example retrieving all aspects connected to experiences of not feeling safe.

FINDING INNER PEACE AND ACCESSING THE POWER OF NOW:

The infinity symbol reflects the Hermetic Principle of Rhythm as it swings to both sides and always returns to its centre.

Go into your zero-point. Stretch out your arms to both sides. Invite an infinity symbol into your energetic system with its centre located in the middle of your heart chakra and the loops reaching out through your arms to your hands. Energetically first follow the left loop and then the right loop. Can you see, sense or feel how you are being pulled first by the left side and then by the right side? Now come to stillness in the infinity symbol's centre in the middle of your heart chakra where the opposite loops co-exist in absolute equilibrium with each other. Do you feel the stillness in your heart? Do you feel present in the here and now? Know that you can neutralise the effects of the outside pulls at any time by consciously returning to your centre, your zero-point.

ACCESSING THE QUANTUM FIELD, EXPERIENCING ONENESS AND CREATING NEW EXPERIENCES:

From the zero-point you have access to the quantum field with all its infinite potential. Imagine multidimensional infinity symbols that intersect at one point, the zero-point, rotating through space and time. Set the intention to step into the very intersection of those loops and relax into the flow of life, experiencing life from the perspectives of union and unity. Can you feel, sense or know the oneness within you, and with the outside world? "As above, so below. As within, so without." – The Kybalion[29].

From this level of oneness, you might want to call one of your heart's desires into existence. Let's take the example of inviting a new partner into your life: See, sense or feel two complete, whole, equal-sized circles coming together in an infinity symbol – intersecting in the zero-point where you currently find yourself – and engaging in a beautiful dance with each other.

---

[29] See Chapters 8 and 10 for further references.

# 7.17
# From Competition to Connection and Sharing Your Gifts with the World

Please be aware that you might not feel the energies of the stars with double-digit numbers as strongly as the energies of those with single-digits, due to their collective nature.

**6-pointed star, 10-pointed star, 11-pointed star and 12-pointed star:**

The 6-pointed star, followed by the 12-pointed star, together support you first in centring yourself by connecting vertically to the Earth below and the Sun above, then in expanding your aligned self (horizontally) to the left and right by living your calling and sharing your gifts with the world.

See, sense or feel where your centre is: It could be your navel, your solar plexus and/or the centre of your heart chakra. I prefer to connect with the world from my zero-point in the centre of my heart chakra.

You can jump from the practice with the 6-pointed star directly to the practice with the 12-pointed star. Alternatively, you can gradually prepare the activation of your calling and mastery by first working with the 6-pointed star, then with the 10-pointed star, the 11-pointed star and finally the 12-pointed star in the order presented below. The 10-pointed star supports you in proceeding from the individual to the collective experience, activating unity consciousness. The 11-pointed star helps you prepare for your calling and mastery.

Practices:

## 6-pointed star:

## CENTRING YOURSELF:

Use your personal 6-pointed star where the length of each of the 6 lines corresponds to your height from head to toe. Go into your zero-point. By building a physical version on the ground, seeing it in your mind's eye or feeling/sensing it energetically, step into the centre of your personal 6-pointed star and feel its energy. See, sense or feel your connection to the Earth below through the downward-pointing triangle, breathing into it to make it stronger. See, sense or feel your connection to the Sun above through the upward-pointing triangle and breathe into it to make it stronger. Connect to and feel into your centre in your torso, vertically aligning and centring yourself.

## 10-pointed star:

## ACTIVATING UNITY CONSCIOUSNESS:

Go into your zero-point. Visualise, sense or feel a 5-pointed star within your energy system (you might want to refer back to Chapter 5.1). Ask for your essence represented by this 5-pointed star to be activated within you. Visualise, sense or feel another 5-pointed star outside of you. Set the intention to connect to it. Experience how your own essence meets the essence of someone else, or the essence of the human collective. Can you visualise, sense or feel how the second 5-pointed star connects harmoniously with the first one within you, by forming a 10-pointed star in your energy system? Invite the 10-pointed star to rotate in your energy system for your highest and best good to activate unity consciousness within you. Breathe and relax into the energies.

**11-pointed star:**

## PREPARING YOU FOR YOUR CALLING AND MASTERY:

Go into your zero-point. Set the intention for your journey: Where do you want to go? What do you want to offer to the world? Then take your place behind the steering wheel. Invite an 11-pointed star into your energy system by simply calling it in and asking for its activation. Invite it to rotate in your energy system with the intention of preparing and supporting you on the journey to your calling and mastery. Experience its energy; see its magic; receive its insights, for example on the next steps to take. Be open for wherever the journey takes you, even if it involves a changing of course.

**12-pointed star:**

## ACTIVATING YOUR CALLING AND MASTERY:

Go into your zero-point. See, sense or feel a 12-pointed star in front of you. By intention, step into the centre of your 12-pointed star and feel its energy. Experience your connection to the Earth below through the downward-pointing triangle and your connection to the Sun above through the upward-pointing one. Breathe into this vertical alignment and centre yourself. When you feel aligned with both the above and the below, consciously breathe out from your heart chakra into the triangles on your left and right sides, radiating your light horizontally into the world. Now you have activated your 12-pointed star. Invite the 12-pointed star to rotate in your energy system, activating your calling and mastery. See, sense, feel or know your beneficial impact on other people and in the world at large.

**Diamond:**

The diamond acts as an antenna to receive frequencies and it accelerates and magnifies the impact of the words, emotions, deeds and vibrations you send out.

Practice:

## MAGNIFYING AND TRANSMITTING GRATITUDE:

Go into your zero-point. Feel gratitude for something or someone in your life. Expand the feeling of gratitude through your breath and intention. Then invite a diamond into your energy field, asking it to activate itself and to spin in your energy system and physical body with the intention of magnifying and transmitting the frequency of gratitude into all your cells, chakras, organs and glands. Breathe, focusing on feeling gratitude and relaxing into the experience. When you feel gratitude within your whole being, connect to your pineal gland near the centre of the brain, behind the third eye. Set the intention of sending out the signal and frequency of gratitude into the world through the pineal gland, the transmitter within you, and imagine gratitude frequencies streaming from there into the world. Watch what unfolds in the following days.

The frequency of gratitude powerfully draws more people and situations into your life that you can be grateful for. You can also do the practice with other high vibrational frequencies such as love, peace and joy.

# 7.18
# From a World Out of Balance to Divine Order and Harmony

As mentioned, you might not feel the energies of the stars with double-digit numbers as strongly as those with single-digit numbers, due to their collective nature.

**12-pointed star, 13-pointed star and 14-pointed star:**

You can gradually prepare for a life in alignment with natural and universal cycles and laws on a collective level by first activating this alignment within you on an individual level through the 7-pointed star (see Chapter 7.11). Follow this by working with the 12-pointed, 13-pointed and 14-pointed stars in the order presented below. The 12-pointed star supports you in activating your calling and mastery. The 13-pointed star assists in integrating your mastery, as well as activating your multidimensional DNA and preparing you for an increased overall coherence. The 14-pointed star supports you in activating balance, harmony and coherence with all life.

Practices:

**12-pointed star:**

ACTIVATING YOUR CALLING AND MASTERY:

Please refer to the practice in Chapter 7.17.

**13-pointed star:**

ACTIVATING YOUR MULTIDIMENSIONAL DNA AND INNATE ABILITIES:

Go into your zero-point. Invite a 13-pointed star into your energy system by simply calling it in and asking for its activation. Next, invite it to rotate in your energy system with the intention of supporting you in integrating your mastery and activating your multidimensional DNA and innate abilities. See, sense, feel or know how your inner wisdom and sensitivity increase and how things fall into their natural place. Ask the 13-pointed star to prepare you for a stronger harmony and coherence within and around you.

**14-pointed star:**

ACTIVATING BALANCE, HARMONY AND COHERENCE WITH ALL LIFE:

Go into your zero-point. Imagine a multidimensional 7-pointed star in front of you through visualising, sensing or feeling it. By intention step into this 7-pointed star, asking for its activation and experiencing how it expands in all directions. See, sense, feel or know that you are in flow with all life and that you are spiralling upwards, advancing in alignment with natural and cosmic cycles.

Now visualise, sense or feel a second multidimensional 7-pointed star outside yourself, reflecting this internal harmony back to you. Invite the external star into your energy field and see, sense or feel how it harmoniously connects with the first 7-pointed star within you by forming a 14-pointed star in your energy system. Ask the 14-pointed star to activate itself and to rotate in your energy system with the intention of strengthening your experience of balance, harmony and coherence with all life. Breathe and experience the overall balance and alignment with natural and universal cycles within you.

**Metatron's Cube:**

Metatron's Cube is a suitable geometric form to support you in manifesting your ideas and visions that are in alignment with your soul plan.

Practice:

PLANTING SEEDS AND EXPLORING THE FRUITS OF A NEW LIFE INSIDE AND OUT:

It might be useful to do some of the practices in Chapters 7.8 and 7.10 first to gain clarity around your higher purpose and what you want to create from your heart.

Go into your zero-point. Set up a huge Metatron's Cube in front of you. You can do it physically by drawing the corresponding circles of the Fruit of Life (the basic structure of Metatron's Cube, see Figure 31) and lines on the ground, by using a printout of Metatron's Cube (see Figure 32) to step onto, or energetically by intention and through your mind's eye. Step into the heart of Metatron's Cube, the inner circle, and ask for Metatron's Cube to be activated.

Breathe and connect to your soul. In connection with your soul start planting seeds for your new life in the inner ring of circles. From the centre of Metatron's Cube step into each of the six inner circles in turn and tune in: What are the (six main) elements of your new life which are in alignment with your soul? Write down a few words for each of the six circles of the inner ring. You can also use symbols or images instead of words.

Once you have completed the inner ring, connect to the outer ring of circles. From the centre of Metatron's Cube step into each inner circle in turn and from there into the corresponding outer circle. Tune in: What kinds of fruits does this element of your new life bear for a new collective human experience? Write or place the corresponding words, images or symbols in each of the circles of the outer ring.

At the end, step back into the centre of Metatron's Cube. See, sense, feel and know – use as many senses as possible – how the seeds you have just planted are starting to grow and how your new life takes form and bears fruit in your inner and outer experience. Is there a word, symbol or image emerging for the central circle? Ask Metatron's Cube to support you in bringing your seeds to fruition.

**Strengthening divine order and harmony with the dodecahedron, the Cosmic Egg and the Flower of Life**

I frequently use the dodecahedron, the Cosmic Egg and the Flower of Life in the context of strengthening the experience of divine order and harmony on individual and collective levels.

Practices:

**Dodecahedron:**

INFUSING DIVINE ORDER AND HARMONY INTO A SITUATION OR PLACE:

Go into your zero-point. Tune into a conflictive situation or a physical place you want to upgrade (house, area, city, Earth). Invite a dodecahedron vortex into this situation or place for the highest and best good of all concerned: "I call for the installation and activation of a dodecahedron vortex in this situation/this place to infuse divine order and harmony into it for the highest and best good of all concerned." Breathe, close your eyes and notice what you perceive.

**Cosmic Egg:**

## STRENGTHENING DIVINE ORDER AND HARMONY IN A SITUATION, RELATIONSHIP OR PLACE:

Go into your zero-point. Bring a physical or energetic Cosmic Egg into any situation, relationship or place, ask it to activate itself and rotate with the intention of strengthening divine order and harmony there for the highest and best good of all concerned. If you infuse a physical Cosmic Egg into a specific location, you might want to walk around in that location with the Cosmic Egg in your hands and/or deposit it in the specific location after this practice. Roll your physical Cosmic Egg around in your hands or keep visualising, sensing or feeling a rotating golden Cosmic Egg, emanating its energies and codes into that situation, relationship or location until you see, sense, feel or know that the energies and frequencies reflect divine order and harmony.

## CONTRIBUTING TO HIGHER VIBRATIONS ON EARTH:

Go into your zero-point. Hold or imagine a golden Cosmic Egg in your hands, asking for its activation and rotation. Offer the high vibrational codes of the golden Cosmic Egg to the magnetic grid systems of Earth, to any kinds of systems on Earth and/or to humanity for the highest and best good of all concerned, with the intention of facilitating higher vibrations on Earth and the re-birth of Earth as a golden planet. Breathe, close your eyes and notice what you perceive.

While working with the Cosmic Egg in this way, I saw how it opened up and transmuted closed-loop systems on Earth that did not serve us anymore, bringing in space, expansion and new higher vibrational energies and systems.

**Flower of Life:**

## SUPPORTING THE EXPERIENCE OF DIVINE ORDER, HARMONY AND PEACE:

Go into your zero-point. See, sense or feel a multidimensional unbounded Flower of Life in front of you. Ask for its activation and set the intention to infuse the Flower of Life into an energetic system, a geographical area or a situation for the highest and best good of all concerned. Ask it to support the experience of divine order, harmony and peace. Breathe and let the energies do their work while focusing on the experience of divine order, harmony and peace in that context.

## CLAIMING YOUR GENETIC SEAT AND STRENGTHENING DIVINE ORDER IN YOUR FAMILY SYSTEM:

Use the Flower of Life as a basis for your genetic family system. You are in the circle in the centre of the Flower of Life, which represents your genetic seat. Behind you, are your ancestors – ideally (representing divine order) each one in his or her circle representing his or her genetic seat. Your female ancestors stand behind you on the left, starting with your mother. Behind your mother, are her mother on the left and her father on the right and so on. Your male ancestors stand on the right behind you, starting with your father. Behind your father, there are his mother on the left and his father on the right and so on.

Your siblings are at your left and right sides in order of age, starting from the eldest on the very left up to the youngest on the very right. In front of you, there are your future generations, starting with your children in order of age from left to right.

Go into your zero-point. Connect to your genetic family system and activate it by intention. See, sense or feel the Flower of Life of your genetic family system in front of you, behind you and around you. Energetically step into the innermost centre of the

Flower of Life and claim your genetic seat by intention. Connect from your zero-point to the zero-points of the members of your family. You might want to go backwards and forwards for seven generations. Ask each family member in your genetic system to take his or her respective genetic seat in divine order. See, sense, feel or know if certain family members are not in their seats and might need support. If this is the case, ask that family member what he or she needs to take their seat and lend your support, if appropriate. Preferably keep going until all the family members – the unborn children included – have taken their genetic seats in your genetic Flower of Life, reflecting divine order in your genetic family system. You can send waves of light and love from your zero-point to your ancestors and future generations through the Flower of Life and have them returned to you.[30]

---

[30]  This practice was inspired by Damien Wynne's work with genetic core family systems based on the Flower of Life (see references to his work in Chapter 10).

# 7.19
# From Separation to Oneness

Please be aware that you might not feel the energies of the stars with double-digit numbers as strongly as the energies of the stars with single-digit numbers, due to their collective nature.

**14-pointed star, 15-pointed star and 16-pointed star:**

You can gradually prepare for oneness by working first with the 14-pointed star, then the 15-pointed star and finally the 16-pointed star in the order presented below. The 14-pointed star supports you in activating balance, harmony and coherence with all life. The 15-pointed star helps you to integrate the overall coherence and flow of life and prepares you for oneness. The 16-pointed star supports you in experiencing oneness.

Practices:

**14-pointed star:**

ACTIVATING BALANCE, HARMONY AND COHERENCE WITH ALL LIFE:

Please refer to the practice in Chapter 7.18.

**15-pointed star:**

INTEGRATING FLOW OF LIFE AND PREPARING FOR ONENESS:

Go into your zero-point. Invite a 15-pointed star into your energy system by simply calling it in and asking for its activation. Invite it to rotate in your energy system with the intention of supporting you in integrating overall coherence and flow of life and in activating compassion with all life within you. Breathe and relax into the energies. See, sense, feel or know how your flow with life and your compassion increases. Ask the 15-pointed star to prepare you for the experience of oneness.

## 16-pointed star:

ACTIVATING ONENESS:

Go into your zero-point. Visualise, sense or feel a multidimensional 8-pointed star in front of you. Invite it into your energy system and ask for its activation and rotation within, around and through you. Breathe and experience the expansion of your consciousness. Ask for Christ Consciousness to be birthed within you and experience the connection to everything and everyone.

After a while imagine a second multidimensional 8-pointed star outside of you and invite it into your energy system. Visualise, sense or feel how it harmoniously connects with the first 8-pointed star by forming a 16-pointed star within your energy field. See, sense or feel how the compassion and light within you meets the compassion and light of someone else or of the human collective. Invite the 16-pointed star to rotate in your energy system with the intention of supporting you in experiencing oneness with all life.

## 17-pointed star and 18-pointed star:

After playing with the 16-pointed star, you might want to continue with completing old collective paradigms and stepping out of the old "matrix" supported by the 17-pointed star and the 18-pointed star.

**17-pointed star:**

## INTEGRATING ONENESS AND PREPARING TO LEAVE OLD COLLECTIVE PARADIGMS:

Go into your zero-point. Invite a 17-pointed star into your energy system by simply calling it in and asking for its activation. Invite it to rotate in your energy system with the intention of supporting you in integrating your experience of oneness with all life. Ask the 17-pointed star to help you prepare to leave old collective paradigms. Breathe and relax into the energies.

**18-pointed star:**

## DETACHING FROM OLD COLLECTIVE PARADIGMS AND THE OLD "MATRIX":

Go into your zero-point. Visualise, sense or feel a multidimensional 9-pointed star in front of you. Invite it into your energy system and ask for its activation and rotation within, around and through you. See, sense, feel or know how your own old paradigms and patterns are completed. Ask the 9-pointed star for support in detaching from old patterns, beliefs and energies that do not serve you anymore. See, sense, feel or know how your freedom increases.

After a while invite a second multidimensional 9-pointed star into your energy system. Visualise, sense or feel how it harmoniously connects with the first 9-pointed star by forming a multidimensional 18-pointed star within you. Invite the 18-pointed star to rotate in your energy system with the intention of freeing you from old collective paradigms that no longer serve you. See, sense, feel or know how those unwanted paradigms start crumbling within you. Can you feel your detachment from the old "matrix"?

### 22-pointed star, 24-pointed star and 33-pointed star:

Are you now ready to step into new paradigms and experience oneness on a universal level? Then continue with the 22-pointed star, the 24-pointed star and the 33-pointed star.

Practices:

### 22-pointed star:

ACTIVATING THE UNIVERSE WITHIN YOU:

Go into your zero-point. Invite a multidimensional 22-pointed star into your energy system and ask for its activation. Invite it to rotate in your energy system for your highest and best good. Breathe. Experience its energy; see its magic; feel the expansion of your essence from your zero-point through your body into your place, your country and planet Earth. See, sense, feel or know that the universe, with all its stars, is within you. You have access to universal energies and wisdom all the time because it is all inside you.

### 24-pointed star:

EXPERIENCING ONENESS WITH THE WHOLE UNIVERSE:

Go into your zero-point. Visualise, sense or feel a multidimensional 8-pointed star in front of you. Invite it into your energy system and ask for its activation and rotation within, around and through you. Breathe and experience the expansion of your consciousness. Ask for Christ Consciousness to be birthed within you and experience the connection to everything and everyone.

After a while, imagine a second multidimensional 8-pointed star outside yourself and invite it into your energy system. Visualise, sense or feel how it harmoniously connects with the first 8-pointed star by forming a 16-pointed star within your energy field. Ask for the activation and rotation of the 16-pointed star in your energy system. See, sense or feel how the compassion and light within you meets the compassion and light of someone else or of the human collective.

A little later, imagine a third multidimensional external 8-pointed star and invite it into your energy system. Visualise, sense or feel how it harmoniously connects with the 16-pointed star by forming a 24-pointed star within your energy field. See, sense or feel how the compassion and light within you meets the compassion and light of the whole universe.

Invite the 24-pointed star to activate itself and to rotate in your energy system with the intention of supporting you in experiencing oneness with the whole universe and all of existence. Breathe.

**33-pointed star:**

GO WHERE NOT MANY HAVE GONE BEFORE YOU – AND BE OPEN FOR SURPRISES:

Go into your zero-point. Visualise, sense or feel a huge multidimensional 33-pointed star in front of you. You might experience it as a standalone star with 33 points or as three 11-pointed stars coming together as one. Set the intention to step into the centre of the 33-pointed star, ask it to activate itself and to rotate within, around and through your energy system for your highest and best good. Breathe. Experience its energies and let it reveal its magic to you. From your zero-point feel or sense how the consciousness of the human collective expands through you to planet Earth, to our solar system, to the Milky Way galaxy and from there to the whole universe. See, sense, feel or know that the ALL THAT IS is expressing through you. Tune in: What becomes possible now? Be open to what emerges.

## 7.20
## Invitation to a MER-KA-BA Journey
## with the Three Magi

Figure 94: MER-KA-BA

I invite you to join me on a journey with the Three Magi:[31] The Three Magi are multidimensional beings, alchemists with a connection to other dimensions, who offer their gifts to humanity. They followed the Star of Bethlehem to find baby Jesus.

Connect to your own Merkaba first. Let me repeat the practice of how to activate your personal Merkaba:

Go into your zero-point and breathe. Set the intention to build your personal Merkaba field energetically around you, feeling the energy. Focus on the living intelligent light field in and around you. See, sense or feel the Earth tetrahedron that grounds you and see, sense or feel the Sun tetrahedron connecting you to the universe. See, sense or feel how both poles come together as one in your torso, aligning with the Earth and the Sun at the same time. Breathe deeply with

---

[31]  I have been inspired for this MER-KA-BA journey by Panache Desai's powerful meditation with the Three Magi. You can access it for free once you create a free member account on his website at:
https://members.panachedesai.com/gifts-magi-program.

the intention of expanding and experiencing your light body. Your Merkaba is activated.

Now invite in the Three Magi. See, sense, feel or know how the Three Magi come to you – one after the other – offering their gifts. Invite the gifts into your body and energy system for your highest and best good and relax into the experience.

- Melchior (MER), representing the divine universal *Light* and Source of all life, offers gold which serves to purify the body and energy systems, freeing us from old and outdated energies and paradigms. Invite the gold in. See, sense or feel how the gold comes into your body and energy field, purifying them. The gold supports humanity and each and every one of us in remembering and embodying our highest possible light and wisdom in every moment. It activates Christ Consciousness – the compassion with all life – within us.

- Kaspar (KA), representing the *Life Force* animating our bodies, offers frankincense which serves to free us from mental limitations and constraints such as thoughts and desires rooted in fear, lack and survival. Invite the frankincense in. See, sense or feel how the frankincense comes into your mind and liberates it from mental limitations and constraints. The frankincense supports humanity and each and every one of us in expanding our consciousness so that we can embody our Higher Selves more fully.

- Balthazar (BA), representing the *Soul*, offers myrrh which serves to unite the energies of heaven and Earth through our body, our human form. Invite the myrrh in. See, sense or feel how the myrrh supports you in unifying polarities and experiencing wholeness within you. The myrrh supports humanity and each and every one of us in ending our experience of separation and in living from Christ Consciousness – in union with ALL THAT IS – now and forevermore.

Bask in the energies. See, sense, feel or know how the three aspects of the MER-KA-BA trinity come together and merge within you, how your physical body becomes luminous, how your consciousness expands and how your human self and your Higher Self come together as one: Christ Consciousness is now born within you, the pure universal love that IS YOU at the deepest level of your being.

If you want to enjoy this MER-KA-BA journey with the Three Magi as a guided activation to anchor and ground these gifts within you, the audio is on my website, as a gift to you, under the following link: https://www.sabinekruse.com/book/ (join my newsletter and then enter the code: *TRUESELF)*.

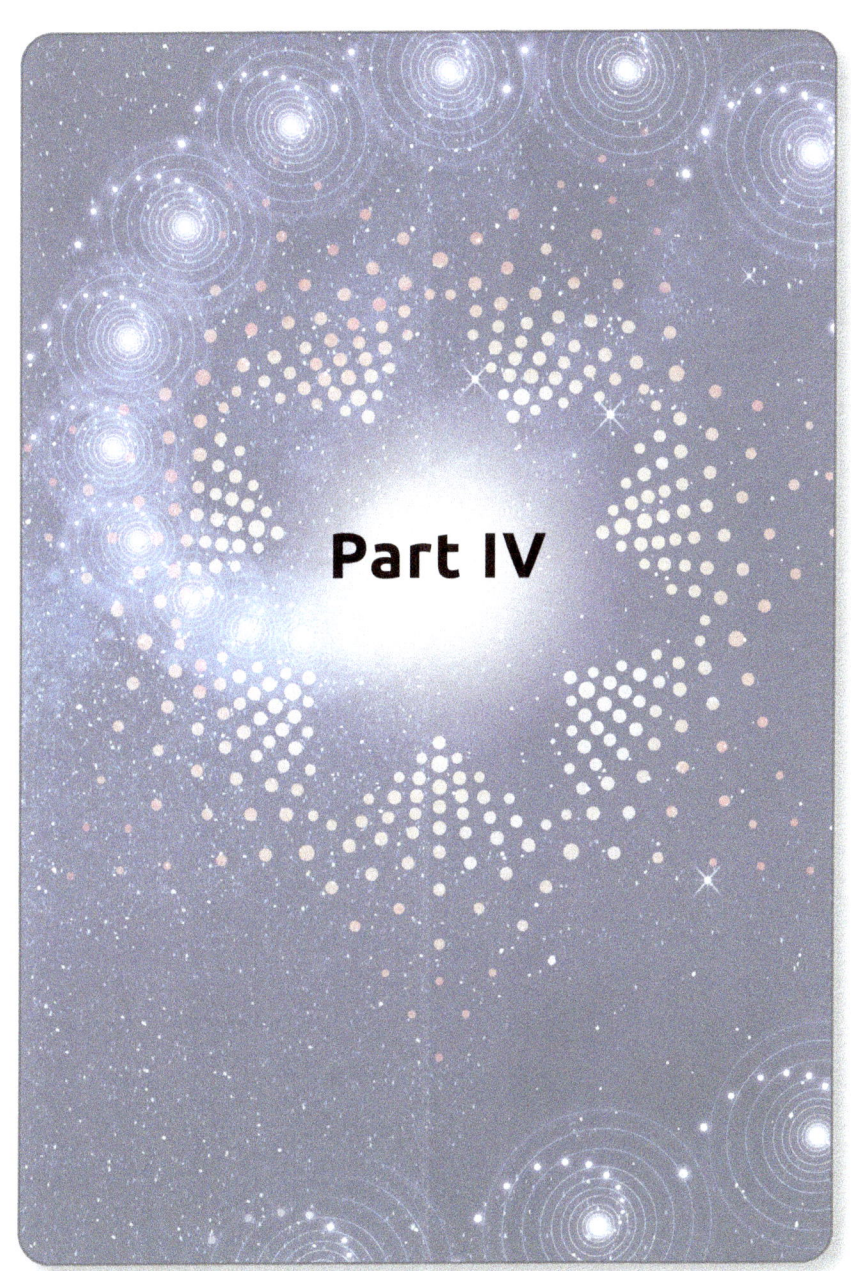

# Part IV

# Chapter 8

# Sacred Geometry Series on the 7 Hermetic Principles

Figure 95: Vesica Piscis at Chalice Well in Glastonbury/England

On the following pages, you will find a synopsis of my sacred geometry series on the "7 Hermetic Principles" posted on my Instagram account from 1.11.2019 until 13.1.2020 and available on my website in a document for you as readers of this book.[32] I invite you to dive into this 9-week series and to be inspired by the universal laws and the accompanying frequencies of the sacred geometries.

---

[32] https://www.instagram.com/sacredgeometryexperience/ and https://www.sabinekruse.com/book/ (join my newsletter and then enter the code: *TRUESELF*)

## Are you aware of the 7 Universal Laws and how they affect and shape your life?

The operation of our universe is based on certain mechanisms: The 7 Hermetic Principles are universal laws that show us how to live in alignment and harmony with the universe and ALL THAT IS. They are teachings from Hermes Trismegistus written down in the "Kybalion"[33] and used in Ancient Egypt and Ancient Greece.

First of all, I invite you to connect with the energy of the 7-pointed star, go for a walk and gaze into the stars, feeling your connection to nature and to the universe. The 7-pointed star supports you in regaining your internal balance and harmony and also with the elements around you. It reflects the cyclical attributes and inherent rhythms of creation, nature and the cosmos. Choose one of the practices in Chapter 7.11 with your favourite version of the 7-pointed star and see, sense, feel or know that you are in the flow with all life and in alignment with natural and cosmic cycles.

## I. The Principle of Mentalism: "THE ALL is MIND; The Universe is Mental." – *The Kybalion.*

Spirit = THE ALL (THAT IS) = an infinite living Mind, created a universe that is mental and subject to 7 universal laws. The material universe is a thought in the mind of Spirit. This principle of mentalism is the overall principle and has many implications. We create our realities, among other things, through our thoughts and beliefs. I invite you to listen to your thoughts and focus them on what your soul wants to create. Energy follows (focused) thought and manifests after a while.

The octahedron is a suitable geometric form to clear mental confusion and to activate clarity and focus within you. You will find corresponding practices in Chapter 7.5.

---

[33] Three Initiates: The Kybalion – a study of the hermetic philosophy of Ancient Egypt and Greece, USA, Martino Publishing Mansfield Centre, 2016

"While All is in THE ALL, it is equally true that THE ALL is in All." – *The Kybalion.*

Spirit is in us – we are co-creators. Let the sphere – the symbol of creation – assist you with creating from the depth of your being (see Chapter 7.10).

## II. The Principle of Correspondence: "As above, so below; as below, so above." – *The Kybalion.*

There is harmony and correspondence between the various planes of existence. The perceived differences in size make it difficult to see that the phenomena of the macrocosm are equal to those of the microcosm. When we learn to understand the microcosm, we can apply this knowledge to the macrocosm, allowing us to see the bigger picture of life, and vice versa. I invite you to perceive your world with new eyes and to look out for the correspondence and interconnectedness of life phenomena. What do you notice? Can you see the structure of a tree in its leaf?

## "As within, so without; as without, so within."

Our inner life, conscious or unconscious, is reflected in our outer manifest world – and vice versa. Look at what is happening around you and you will find out what is happening within you. We live in a vibrational universe. Our state is informing our reality. The more we shift into the vibration of love and inner peace, the more we can experience that in our reality. What do you want to experience today?

## III. The Principle of Vibration: "Nothing rests; everything moves; everything vibrates." – *The Kybalion.*

Change is the only constant in life. Not a single thing or emotion is permanent. Accept change as a natural phenomenon and go with the flow, as resistance is painful. We are wired for change. The principle of vibration is the law that shows us the way to change our lives.

Differences between various manifestations of matter, energy, mind and Spirit result from varying rates of vibration. Spirit is at the highest pole of vibration whereas certain gross forms of matter are at the lowest vibrational pole. Which frequency are you vibrating at?

Experience your Merkaba field through practices in Chapters 7.7 and 7.9 or connect to the Stargate[34], a complex pyramidal sacred geometry structure creating a strong, multidimensional energy field, to raise your energy levels and vibration.

**IV. The Principle of Polarity: "Everything is dual; everything has poles; everything has its pair of opposites; like and unlike are the same." – *The Kybalion.***

We live in a polar universe. Pairs of opposites exist everywhere. You breathe in and you breathe out. Spirit and Matter are two poles of the same thing. Everything and everyone are vibrating somewhere along that line of polarisation. The human experience is a game of balancing polarities. The more you are willing to feel everything and embrace your pain, the more you increase your ability to feel peace and joy.

I invite you to be aware of the polarity within and around you. Use the Vesica Piscis (see Figure 95 and Chapter 7.13), the symbol of duality, to explore the relationship between the masculine and the feminine within you.

For a moment, let's look at your perception of polarity: Is your glass half empty or half full?

There is no absolute standard – it's all a matter of degree. At which point do you perceive your glass to be full rather than empty? We can shift from one state of polarity to the next. Polarities are the same in nature but different in degree. That means: You can shift from

---

34 https://www.thestargateexperienceacademy.com/ev_-_what_is_the_stargate

empty to full and from cold to heat but you cannot shift from empty to heat.

Let's take the example of shifting from conflict to peace. I invite you to feel into a situation of conflict. Can you feel it? Now bring in the frequency of compassion, followed by the frequency of understanding, then the frequency of forgiveness. Can you feel the vibrational shift towards peace?

**V. The Principle of Rhythm: "Everything flows out and in; everything has its tides; all things rise and fall." – *The Kybalion*.**

There is a pendulum-like movement in everything between the two poles, which exist in accordance with the Principle of Polarity:

• Swing backwards and forwards
• Rising and sinking
• Action and reaction

You notice it in the creation and destruction of stars, the tides of the ocean, the rise and fall of companies and football clubs, as well as in your own mental and emotional states.

Birth, growth, maturity, decline, death and then birth again…

Become aware of your mental and emotional states: How far does the pendulum swing in your moods, thoughts and emotions? Use a practice with the infinity symbol in Chapter 7.16 to return to your centre and know that by staying in your centre, you may escape the effects of the swinging pendulum.

The pendulum ever swings but the observer does not. Who do you identify with?

**VI. The Principle of Cause and Effect:** "Every Cause has its Effect; every Effect has its Cause; everything happens according to Law; Chance is but a name for law not recognized; there are many planes of causation, but nothing escapes the Law." – *The Kybalion.*

Chance does not exist. All events happen according to Law. The Principle of Cause and Effect states that there is a cause for every effect and an effect from every cause. Every thought we think and every action we take have their direct and indirect results, which fit into the great global chain of Cause and Effect.

When you raise your vibration and enter higher planes of consciousness, you can consciously set the cause rather than become the undesired effect. Life then happens FOR YOU, rather than TO YOU. Set the cause in motion by being that what you wish to see in the world. Then sit back and watch the ripple effects.

One aspect of the Principle of Cause and Effect is the Law of Attraction. When you plant a desired outcome in your heart and nurture it with your thoughts, emotions and actions, you draw more and more of it into your life. Which seed are you planting today?

**VII. The Principle of Gender:** "Gender is in everything; everything has its Masculine and Feminine Principles; Gender manifests on all planes." – *The Kybalion.*

GENDER – the masculine and feminine principles – is present and active in everything. You find it in the male/female sex and in positive/negative poles of electrified or magnetised matter. Gender manifests on all planes – physical, mental and even spiritual. It is necessary for the generation of ideas, the procreation of new beings as well as the creation of objects and third entities.

On the mental plane, the Principle of Gender looks like this: Your masculine aspect directs his will towards your feminine aspect. Your feminine aspect then starts creating thoughts, ideas, concepts, beliefs and feelings in alignment with the codes she has received. The codes reflect a certain consciousness – your ego mind, the divine mind or even the will of another person who is influencing you. Which consciousness is reflected in your mental creations?

Explore the masculine and feminine principles within you through the Yin and Yang symbol or the Vesica Piscis.

**How to be in flow with nature and the universe**

My three favourite practical teachings are:

- Raise your vibration and live a more fulfilled life.
- Consciously shift from one degree of polarity to the next until you are vibrating at the desired frequency.
- Be the change you wish to see in the world.

What are your favourites?

We have explored the seven rules of the universal game. You are the one who is playing it. Have you developed a new awareness which will be helpful to you?

# Chapter 9

# Final Words

Figure 96: 10-pointed star surrounded by 5-pointed stars –
Design on a ceiling in the Royal Alcázar of Seville/Spain

Writing this book has taken me on a fascinating journey.

After my meditations with information on the energetic properties
of sacred geometry shapes and forms, it was quite a process for me
to decide which geometric shapes and forms to include in this book.
In the end, I opted for the foundational ones such as the sphere, the
five Platonic solids, the Merbaka, Metatron's Cube and the Flower
of Life as they are widely used and known and powerful in their own
rights. Being surrounded by a variety of sacred geometry stars in
and around Granada/Spain, and having received insights on how to
use them, encouraged me to focus on the stars (from the 5-pointed

star to the 33-pointed star) in a chapter of their own. Out of the many sacred symbols, I chose to elaborate on my favourite one – the Egyptian Ankh.

It was only towards the end of writing this book, after telepathically receiving Thoth's message to the reader, that I understood that we had activated our 12-strand DNA during the ceremony in 2015 (see Preface) and that joining the 12 pieces allowed for the emergence of a new 13th entity – a perfect human being with all of his or her innate abilities activated. The purpose of this ceremony was as a contribution towards making ancient wisdom and abilities available again for these exciting and equally challenging times of change on Earth. It was an activation of the "perfect" human. When we embody him or her, we can truly express our unique genius. I will share more insights and frequencies related to embodying and expressing our highest potentials in my next books. I also came to realise that my re-activated gift was related to sacred geometry.

Something else happened during my own first edit of the book: I had thought the book was complete, only to find out that I needed to go through another round of editing and doing my own practices in order to fully anchor the frequencies and codes in my body and in the book. I went through my own unique process to create the results in me which the book is all about: activating my highest potential with sacred geometry through remembering my True Self. Since then, many puzzle pieces have fallen into place and synchronicities appeared everywhere.

What I love about sacred geometry is its beauty, simplicity and efficiency as well as its alchemical power. We can simply immerse ourselves in the natural frequencies and codes inherent in sacred geometry, thereby remembering and activating our divine blueprint within. In this way, we quickly experience the results of transformation in an empowering way.

How has engaging with sacred geometry, as well as the awareness and practices from this book, benefitted me?

- Using the knowledge about the energetic qualities of different sacred geometry shapes and forms has allowed me to design my own tailor-made sacred geometry symbols for specific purposes (such as self-love, freedom and purpose) for clients and my own work.
- I've gained freedom from old limitations on an emotional level and from disempowering thoughts, beliefs and habits. For example, I used to feel angry and frustrated when things didn't go the way I (my personality) wanted. Now, I'm much more at peace with myself and with whatever is unfolding in my life.
- I've moved away from conformity and from behaving in a way people want or expect me to, towards expressing my truth and living my authentic nature.
- My life has become much more fulfilling through following my heart and soul rather than my mind.

I know that freedom, authenticity and fulfilment are possible for you as well.

I wish to close with an activation of the sacred geometry inherent in each and every one of us and to support you in remembering your True Self.

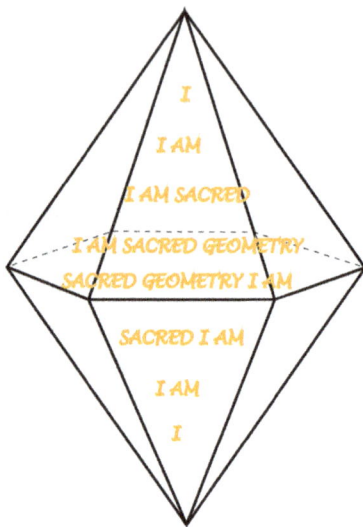

*I*

*I AM*

*I AM SACRED*

*I AM SACRED GEOMETRY*

*SACRED GEOMETRY I AM*

*SACRED I AM*

*I AM*

*I*

Figure 97: Final sacred geometry activation diamond

**Final activation:**

Go into your zero-point in the middle of your heart chakra. Take a few deep breaths and connect to your True Self, to your "I AM PRESENCE". Focus on the diamond depicted above (see Figure 97). Set the intention to energetically step into the diamond and ask for the activation of its crystalline codes and the initiation of the corresponding alchemical process within you – the metamorphosis from your identity/personality to your True Self. Invite this diamond to rotate and spin within, around and through you with the intention of activating the sacred geometry within, of attuning you to the golden ratio both in and around you, as well as with the intention of remembering your True Self. Breathe, relax and bask in the energies.

When you feel or know the time has come, set the intention to radiate your True Self, the love that you are, out into the world and the universe through the many facets of the diamond. Let the diamond reflect your True Self back to you. See, sense, feel or know that your True Self is all there is, all there ever was and all there ever will be. And so it is.

# Chapter 10

# Bibliography and Useful Links

Figure 98: The Egyptian Ankh – the key of life

**Printed Sources**

Beutel, Andreas: Die Blume des Lebens und der Quantenraum – Eine Einführung in die Heilige Geometrie, DVD, Germany, Koha-Verlag GmbH, 2011 (German Edition)

Carroll, Lee: Kryon – The 12 layers of DNA (An esoteric study of the mastery within), USA, Platinum Publishing House, 2010

Desai, Panache: You are enough – revealing the soul to discover your power, potential, and possibility, USA, HarperCollins, 2020

Emoto, Masaru: The hidden messages in water, USA, Atria Books, 2005

Hough, Jennifer: Unstuck – the physics of getting out of your own way, USA, I Fly Publishing, 2022

Janosh: Wake up your DNA! The universal language of sacred geometry, the Netherlands, Janosh Art, 2010

Lipton, Bruce H.: The biology of belief: unleashing the power of consciousness, matter & miracles, USA, Hay House, 10th anniversary edition, 2016

Mitchell, John and Brown, Allan: How the world is made: the story of creation according to sacred geometry, USA, Inner Traditions, 2012

Ruland, Jeanne and Ferenz, Gudrun: Die Heilige Geometrie der platonischen Körper, Germany, Schirner Verlag, 2014 (German Edition)

Ruland, Jeanne: Merkaba – Die Aktivierung des Lichtkörpers für die Neue Zeit, Germany, Schirner Verlag, 2016 (German Edition)

Stelzl, Diethard: Heilige Geometrie – die Matrix unserer Welt, Germany, Schirner Verlag, 2016 (German Edition)

Sutton, Daud: Islamic design – a genius for geometry, UK, Wooden Book Ltd, 2007

Three Initiates: The Kybalion – a study of the hermetic philosophy of Ancient Egypt and Greece, USA, Martino Publishing Mansfield Centre, 2016

Wynne, Damien and Devi, Janin: Family constellation on the DNA/genetic-level, audio book, Germany, HOFA GmbH, 2016

## Web Sources

Braden, Gregg: Water Vibration and Sacred Geometry, https://www.youtube.com/watch?v=4p7PFHL5W54, 2014, last visited on 29 March 2023

Desai, Panache: for meditations and support to experience limitless possibilities as well as for the meditation with the Three Magi (see Chapter 7.20): https://www.panachedesai.com, last visited on 29 March 2023

Forum Synergie with Dr. Hans Hein: synergy model of tetrahedral intelligences, https://www.forum-synergie.de/Artikel-Downloads/Die-Zukunft-des-Gehirns/, figure 2, last visited on 29 March 2023 (in German)

Grant, Robert Edward: for background information and illustration of sacred geometry and related topics, https://www.instagram.com/robertedwardgrant/, last visited on 29 March 2023

HeartMath Institute: for information on the power and impact of the heart field, https://www.heartmath.org, last visited on 29 March 2023

Jain 108 Academy: for information and courses on sacred geometry from a mathematical and philosophical perspective, https://jain108academy.com, last visited on 29 March 2023

Janosh: for sacred geometry activations and art, https://www.janosh.com/en/, last visited on 29 March 2023

Metaforms with Gail and Gregory Hoag: for sacred geometry objects and tutorials, https://iconnect2all.com/products/metaforms/, last visited on 29 March 2023

Office Masaru Emoto: Science of water, https://www.masaru-emoto.net/en/, last visited on 29 March 2023

OmniGeometry: Sacred geometry designer software, https://www.omnigeometry.com, last visited on 29 March 2023

Phyllis Krystal Foundation: for a method of cutting cords that bind, https://www.phylliskrystal.com/method/, last visited on 29 March 2023

Quintin, Jonathan: for sacred geometry (photos), https://attunetocosmos.com, last visited on 29 March 2023

Resonance Science Foundation (founder: Haramein, Nassim): for quantum physics and scientific evidence on the interconnectedness of life, https://www.resonancescience.org, last visited on 29 March 2023

The Wide Awakening with Jennifer Hough: for the innate abilities home study and other programmes to thrive, https://thewideawakening.com, last visited on 29 March 2023

Chapter 11

# Outlook on Feminine Sacred Geometry

# The Inner Path to New Earth

Figure 99: Heart leaf

**There is so much more to come ...**

In the journey through this book much has been shared that is potentially life-changing when used in truth and continuity – and yet there is still more to come. My second book will focus on sacred geometry with feminine attributes to provide support in embodying the inner qualities required for New Earth, a glimpse of which follows.

## The return of Pi ($\pi$)

Humanity is currently entering a new phase in its evolution which I will call "New Earth". More light frequencies will arrive on planet Earth from our Sun and the cosmos, facilitating our memory of the truth of who we are and the embodiment of our highest potential. We'll see many lightful changes in human-made structures and systems. In this "New Earth", feminine types of sacred geometry become ever more important. These shapes and forms already exist but are not yet at the forefront of our awareness. "Feminine" in this regard means sacred geometry consisting of softer, rounder and more spherical geometric shapes and forms rather than the sharper, edgier and more solid shapes and forms of triangles, squares and cubes. In general, sacred feminine energies rise within and around us, facilitating the balance of masculine-feminine polarities both internally and externally. In the field of sacred geometry, I am receiving insights about "the return of Pi" and the evolution of geometric shapes and forms into ones with feminine attributes which will strengthen our connection to Mother Earth and her gifts.

## But what is the return of Pi?

Remember Pi from school? The underlying mathematics of circles and spheres contain the sacred infinite number Pi, $\pi = 3.14...$, which – similar to the golden ratio Phi we talked about in Chapter 2 – is all-embracing and reflects divine proportions. Sacred geometry shapes and forms will reflect softer and more circular, spherical and spiral characteristics. Shifting the "masculine" geometries from a square or triangle to a circle and making corresponding adjustments in the other surfaces, creates "feminine" geometric attributes.

Here is an example of the evolution of the "masculine" cube into a "feminine" sphere (see Figure 100).

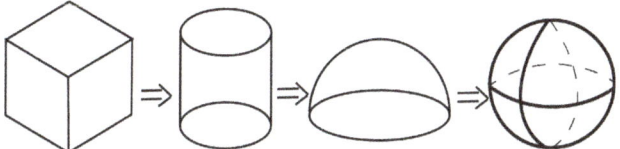

Figure 100: Cube (squares) => Cylinder (circular base
and top) => Dome (spherical) => Sphere

Figure 101 is an example of two similar sacred geometries, one with masculine attributes (pyramid) and one with feminine attributes (cone).

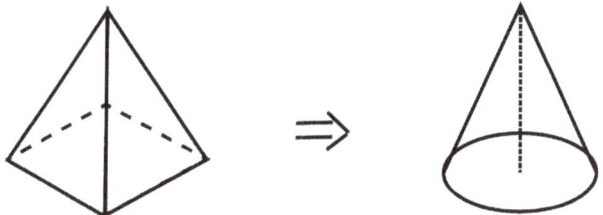

Figure 101: Pyramid (square base with sharp peak)
=> Cone (circular base with softer peak)

Indigenous cultures such as the Native Americans and the Inuit understand the power of circular and spherical structures which is reflected in their cone- and dome-like housing (see Figure 102 Tepee and Figure 103 Igloo) and in their habit of sitting in circles during reunions and ceremonies.

Figure 102: Tepee                    Figure 103: Igloo

In my understanding, this evolution of sacred geometry from very solid shapes and forms – where the presence of the matter can be felt – to more lightful, circular, spherical and spiral shapes and forms reflects our own process of transformation: the gradual shift from our dense carbon-based physical bodies into more lightful, crystalline structures as well as the embodiment of our Higher Selves, our light.

The core of the book is a sacred geometry journey into the Womb of Creation – the inner path to New Earth. I'll guide you on this journey starting with the sacred geometry symbol called Delphi (see Figure 104) which will support you in starting anew from divine scratch, living in flow and being natural.

Figure 104: Delphi

Another highlight will be the activation of magic and miracle conditions through specifically designed sacred geometries which contain the frequencies to activate the miracle conditions and related aspects in you on multidimensional and DNA levels. Also included will be information on the energetic qualities and utilisations of "feminine", non-linear and multidimensional shapes and forms as well as everyday practical exercises to help you activate the feminine qualities within and EMBODY your highest potential with sacred geometry.

# Chapter 12

# Outlook on Combinations and Movements of Sacred Geometry Shapes and Forms

Figure 105: Freedom Symbol

**More gifts to share …**

My third sacred geometry book will focus on combinations and movements of sacred geometry shapes and forms, taking you deeper into the power and mysteries of sacred frequencies and vibrations by combining them in an alchemical way. Certain combinations are particularly powerful, enhancing the effect of the individual shapes or forms and facilitating alchemical processes in our bodies and energetic systems. Add movement to the visual experience and the effects can be felt more strongly, creating balance and harmony between masculine and feminine attributes and qualities and supporting you in expressing and living your highest potential.

## Alchemical process through sacred geometry combinations and movements

Included will be examples of (multidimensional) sacred geometry combinations such as the Cosmic Egg (see Chapter 4.8), the Stargate[35], a complex pyramidal sacred geometry structure, which creates a strong multidimensional energy field and operates as an interdimensional portal, as well as sacred geometry designs based on Metatron's Cube and the (unbounded) Flower of Life. There will be information on their energetic qualities and utilisations as well as inspirational practices.

The Freedom Symbol I designed (see Figure 105) supports you in breaking free from limitations and old paradigms and in spreading your wings to fly. It is based on the unbounded Flower of Life for limitlessness and contains two 9-pointed stars – forming an 18-pointed star – to assist in stepping out of old collective paradigms. The Merkaba harmonises polarities, expanding the light body and aligning with the divine blueprint. The crystalline Pyramid Consciousness symbol (see Figure 107) activates multidimensional abilities and thinking outside the box. In the centre, there are two infinity symbols (for infinite flow) and a butterfly, the symbol of metamorphosis from your old to your new being.

## New paradigms for New Earth related to systems and structures of humanity

I'll also share a series of sacred geometry symbols whose frequencies facilitate the emergence of new paradigms for systems and structures of humanity, which are fundamental for New Earth. By the term "New Earth" I am referring to the new phase of evolution humanity

---

[35] https://www.thestargateexperienceacademy.com/ev_-_what_is_the_stargate

is currently undergoing. Figure 106 contains an example, the Union Symbol, which consists of two pentagrams – symbolising two individual essences – coming together in a 10-pointed star for unity consciousness (see Chapter 5.6) in a fractal pattern. Many versions of the Vesica Piscis at the symbol's rim unite and merge together. Two infinity symbols are at the heart of the symbol – and everything is embedded in a white network representing a toroidal field of connection.

Figure 106: Union Symbol

## Pyramid Consciousness Path – the outer path to New Earth

The heart of this book contains a guided outer path to New Earth, with the support of the Pyramid Consciousness (see starting symbol in Figure 107). I will guide you with the help of specifically designed sacred geometries containing Pyramid Consciousness codes and frequencies as well as related inspirational practices, explaining what Pyramid Consciousness means, which elements the symbols contain and how they can be of service to you and others. On a macro level, Pyramid Consciousness serves as a bridge to other planets and star systems, activating multidimensional abilities in you while, on a micro level, providing bio frequencies and intuitive energies for restoring balance in the body on a cellular level, allowing you to receive wisdom stored within when you are ready.

Figure 107: Pyramid Journey

The information and practices presented in this third book will help balance your masculine and feminine qualities and EXPRESS and LIVE your highest potential with sacred geometry.

# Chapter 13

# Afterword by Thoth

Figure 108: Shining 7-pointed Hermetic Principles Star

I wanted to jump into this final chapter at my beloved number 13, which takes us to a higher level of consciousness. If you have come this far, reading the book and engaging in the practices, this message is for you:

Dear Reader,

Congratulations! Your multidimensional DNA, your highest potential and the universal wisdom within you have been activated!

You now know that you do not need to be ruled by the 7 Hermetic Principles, the 7 rules of the universal game of duality, as you are the one who invented the game and is playing it right now.

Allow me a final question:
Do you identify with the fleeting experiences of the game or with
THE ONE who created it?

*Let your True Self shine brightly!*

And so it is.

With love and gratitude,

THOTH
alias HERMES TRISMEGISTUS

| The 7 Hermetic Principles |
| --- |
| I)    The Principle of Mentalism: THE ALL is MIND; The Universe is Mental. |
| II)    The Principle of Correspondence: As above, so below; as below, so above. |
| III)    The Principle of Vibration: Nothing rests; everything moves; everything vibrates. |
| IV)    The Principle of Polarity: Everything is dual; everything has poles; everything has its pair of opposites; like and unlike are the same. |
| V)    The Principle of Rhythm: Everything flows out and in; everything has its tides; all things rise and fall. |
| VI)    The Principle of Cause and Effect: Every Cause has its Effect; every Effect has its Cause; everything happens according to Law; Chance is but a name for law not recognized; there are many planes of causation, but nothing escapes the Law. |
| VII)    The Principle of Gender: Gender is in everything; everything has its Masculine and Feminine Principles; Gender manifests on all planes. |

# Acknowledgments

I am profoundly grateful to all the people who inspired me personally and through their work during the years of writing this book, notably to Panache Desai for always reminding me who I truly am, to Janosh for awakening the passion for sacred geometry in me and to Jennifer Hough for guiding me back to my heart, as well as to my mentors from higher dimensions such as Thoth, Isis and other light beings.

This book has been graced with a great publishing team: I would like to thank Becky Norwood of Spotlight Publishing House™, Janet Swift, Marigold2k and Danijel Trstenjak for supporting me so compassionately and efficiently in releasing this book to the world as well as Andrea Hylen for her continuous valuable inspiration and assistance during her Writing Incubators. A warm thank you also goes to Danielle M Helms for her fabulous peer review, to all the lovely people who engaged in the book's practices providing precious feedback and endorsements and to those who help spread the word about this book and the power of sacred geometry.

Special thanks go to the creators of OmniGeometry, a sacred geometry software, which allows me to create my graphic designs with ease and beauty.

To my partner and close friends – you know who you are – I give my heartfelt gratitude for all their love and encouragement and for believing in me and this project.

Last but never least, I am eternally and infinitely grateful for the True Self that resides in each and every one of us – the Source of this book, my life and Existence in general.

# Photos and Illustrations

Own graphs: Figures 12, 13, 50

Own images designed with Adobe Illustrator:

Figures 5, 11, 28, 34, 37, 38, 41, 43, 44, 51, 58, 59, 84, 86, 87, 88, 89, 90, 91, 92, 97, 100, 101, 108

Own images designed with OmniGeometry software:

Figures 2, 14, 15, 16, 18, 19, 23, 24, 25, 26, 27, 29, 31, 32, 39, 49, 53, 57, 60, 61, 64, 65, 66, 67, 68, 69, 71, 72, 73, 74, 75, 76, 77, 78, 85, 104, 105, 106, 107

Own photos: Figures 1, 4, 6, 9, 10, 17, 21, 22, 30, 33, 35, 36, 47, 48, 52, 54, 56, 62, 63, 70, 79, 80, 81, 83, 93, 94, 95, 96, 98, 99, 102

Photo by Andres Dallimonti at www.unsplash.com: Figure 20

Photo by Aurelio Jaén Millán: Figure 82

Photos licensed at www.Shutterstock.com:

Figure 3: BasPhoto; Figure 7: Artsiom P; Figure 8: miha de; Figure 40: fluidworkshop; Figure 42: Arnon Polin; Figure 45: Aphelleon; Figure 46: cybermagician; Figure 55: Kichigin; Figure 103: Piotr Piatrouski

# About the Author

Sabine Kruse grew up in Germany with an innate desire to explore the world and the purpose of life. As an economist working for 20 years in the field of development co-operation improving the living conditions of disadvantaged people, she realised the world couldn't be changed from the outside and there was more to life than her corporate job. So began an inner journey of self-awareness and living life from her heart and soul.

Sacred geometry came into Sabine's life at the end of 2014 when, during meditation, she began receiving information on how to use geometric shapes and forms to shift the underlying energetics for everyday issues and create tangible results in daily life. Sabine recorded these insights and experiences, utilising them by means of short practices. Step-by-step, this book took shape. Guided in the use of sacred geometry by Thoth and other mentors from higher realms, Sabine went through a process of freeing herself from limitations and conditioning, returning to her authentic nature. In her passionate desire to go to her very core, she uncovered more of her True Self and in so doing, experiencing more freedom, joy and fulfilment in her life.

Sabine wants that for you as well and so she wrote this book and became a certified Life Coach, Business Coach and Trainer for intercultural competence. Through her writing, coaching, workshops and tailor-made sacred geometry designs she inspires and empowers people to live to their highest potentials.

Living in Southern Spain with her partner, Sabine enjoys travelling, exploring the beauty and diversity of planet Earth, as well as venturing out beyond the known worlds. She loves sunsets on the beach, visiting pyramids and good conversations with friends.

If you'd like to explore this subject further with Sabine, please refer to the links below which include more information and free meditations and activations:

- Website: www.sabinekruse.com
- Instagram: https://www.instagram.com/sacredgeometryexperience/
- YouTube: https://www.youtube.com/@SabineKruse
- LinkedIn: https://www.linkedin.com/in/sabine-kruse-b108aa288/
- Email: info@sabinekruse.com

---

Sacred geometry images for download:

As a reader of this book, you may download and print its sacred geometry images for free in order to use them for the practices described in the book. You will also get free access to the full series on the 7 Hermetic Principles and the MER-KA-BA meditation with the Three Magi.

Visit this section of Sabine's website https://www.sabinekruse.com/book/, join the newsletter, wait for a new page to open, and then enter the code *TRUESELF*.

---

www.ingramcontent.com/pod-product-compliance
Lightning Source LLC
Chambersburg PA
CBHW070910120626
46546CB00001B/204